D1292875

The Stakes of History

The Franz Rosenzweig Lectures in Jewish Theology and History are sponsored by the Program in Judaic Studies at Yale University. The Lectures were established in 1987 by the Estate of Arthur A. Cohen and are named for theologian Franz Rosenzweig.

Other volumes in the Franz Rosenzweig Lecture series available from Yale University Press

Radical Judaism: Rethinking God and Tradition, by Arthur Green

Canon and Creativity: Modern Writing and the Authority of Scripture, by Robert Alter

German Jews: A Dual Identity, by Paul Mendes-Flohr

Freud's Moses: Judaism Terminable and Interminable, by Yosef Hayim Yerushalmi

THE STAKES OF HISTORY

On the Use and Abuse
of Jewish History for Life

DAVID N. MYERS

Yale UNIVERSITY PRESS   New Haven and London

Published with assistance from the Franz Rosenzweig
Lectures in Jewish Theology and History Fund in the
Program in Judaic Studies at Yale University.

Published with assistance from the foundation
established in memory of Calvin Chapin of the
Class of 1788, Yale College.

Yale University Press books may be purchased in
quantity for educational, business, or promotional use.
For information, please e-mail sales.press@yale.edu
(U.S. office) or sales@yaleup.co.uk (U.K. office).

Set in Caslon type by Integrated Publishing Solutions.
Printed in the United States of America.

Library of Congress Control Number: 2017937446
ISBN 978-0-300-22893-9 (hardcover : alk. paper)

A catalogue record for this book is available from the
British Library.

This paper meets the requirements of ANSI/NISO
Z39.48-1992 (Permanence of Paper).

10 9 8 7 6 5 4 3 2 1

To Sondra and Morey Myers

Contents

PREFACE

This book began as an attempt to distill and summarize my thinking about the history of modern Jewish historiography and the role of the modern Jewish historian. I have long been interested in both the production of historical knowledge by modern scholars and the recurrent anxiety over the perceived excesses of a historicist worldview. The moment in which I started to think about this book was beset by its own anxiety, this time over the worth and meaning not only of history but of humanistic inquiry more generally in society. The combination of serious new economic pressures, institutional constraints, and declining student enrollments pushed many—myself included as a historian—to rearticulate what was at stake in our work. Rather than succumb to the despair of the moment, I remained more convinced than ever that historical knowledge and perspective were necessary ingredients in understanding the world we live in and were capable of playing a constructive (though not risk free) role in the wider world—by forging memories that lend meaning to our lives, by complicating received and oversimplified historical narratives, and even by informing policy decisions.

These reflections—and my relatively bullish view of the historian's function—immediately brought me into dialogue with one of the most important books ever written on the vocation and outlook of the Jewish historian, Yosef Hayim Yerushalmi's *Zakhor: Jewish History and Jewish Memory.* The invitation to deliver the Rosenzweig Lectures afforded me the opportunity both to revisit a key pillar of *Zakhor* and to rethink, alongside Yerushalmi, the function and mission of history in the modern age. I elaborate more fully on my connection to *Zakhor* and Professor Yerushalmi in the Introduction and return to both frequently throughout. Suffice it to say that the present book has neither the erudition nor the lyricism of *Zakhor,* though it does share Yerushalmi's description of that volume as "part history, part confession and credo." It is my hope that through this mix of genres I can shed new light on the uses to which history has been put in the past and to which it might profitably be put in the future.

ACKNOWLEDGMENTS

This book emerged out of the invitation of the Yale University Program in Judaic Studies and Professor Steven Fraade to deliver the Franz Rosenzweig Lectures in November 2014. I would like to thank my hosts at Yale for their warm hospitality during the week I spent in New Haven to deliver the lectures: in addition to Steven Fraade, I would like to thank Renee Reed for her gracious assistance in all matters logistical, Elli Stern for his good humor and helpful provocations, and the members of the Judaic Studies community, faculty and students, at Yale. A special debt of appreciation is owed to my dear New Haven friends and interlocutors Anne Dailey, Steve Ecker, and Rabbi Jim Ponet.

Versions of this talk were delivered at the Australian Centre for Jewish Civilization of Monash University. I thank my friend Professor Mark Baker for the kind invitation and hospitality during my delightful stay in Melbourne; I also extend deep appreciation to Helen Midler for attending to every detail relating to my visit with efficiency and humor. I presented ideas related to this book in forums at the Katz Center for Advanced Judaic Studies of the University of Pennsylvania, the CUNY Graduate Center, Lehigh University, and Cardozo Law School. Thanks to Professors Steven Weitzman, Francesca Bregoli, Nitzan Lebovic, and Suzanne Last Stone for their invitations to participate in the stimulating intellectual settings they have created at their institutions. I also thank Professor Magda Teter for a most helpful critique of Chapter 3 at a conference on history and law at Cardozo in September 2016.

Numerous colleagues read this manuscript and improved it considerably. Michael A. Meyer offered typically searching comments on an early version of the manuscript—delivered, per his custom, in forty-eight hours. My thanks go, as well, to Sarah Abrevaya Stein, Michael Berenbaum, Saul Friedlander, David Ellenson, John Efron, Michael Brenner, Ethan Kleinberg, Nitzan Lebovic, and Nomi Stolzenberg for their careful reading. A special thanks goes to my erstwhile student and conversation partner Moshe Lapin, who pored over every page of this book with his sharp eye and wide-ranging knowledge. For invaluable research assistance, I thank Lindsay King, Joshua Meyers, and Talia Graff. Nadav Molchadsky offered very helpful criticism and assistance at early and late stages of the project.

Yale University Press has been a most hospitable home for this book. My thanks go to Jennifer Banks, the Press's editor who oversees publication of the Rosenzweig Lectures series, for her interest, attention, and encouragement. Susan Laity undertook the copyediting of this book with a meticulousness, intelligence, and care that know few peers.

I would like to express my appreciation to Lori and Jim Keir for their friendship and support, as well as to the Sady and Ludwig Kahn Chair in Jewish History which facilitated my work on this project.

Finally, this book is dedicated to my parents, Sondra and Morey Myers, who have avidly followed and encouraged me throughout my career, including in New Haven, to which they dutifully came for the Rosenzweig Lectures. For them, thinking and doing are the necessary and sufficient conditions of a well-lived life. Individually and together, they have modeled the fusing of these two domains in exemplary fashion. I thank them for their ceaseless support, love, and inspiration.

Of course, I alone remain responsible for any errors to be found in the book.

History, Memory, and What Lies in Between

History must be a manual for how to avoid the mistakes of the past; how to break the cycle; a roadmap toward a better world.

BARACK OBAMA, Eulogy for the Rev. Clementa Pinckney, 26 June 2015

There may be no more fitting way to begin this book than to recall the question at the outset of Marc Bloch's *The Historian's Craft:* "Tell me Daddy. What is the use of history?" The poignancy and profundity issue not only from the childlike naïveté in which the question was cloaked but from the circumstances in which it was posed. Bloch wrote his reflections not in the privileged environs of a university, where he had spent the previous twenty-three years of his life, but while serving in the French Resistance. After joining the Resistance in late 1942 or early 1943, Bloch was captured by the Gestapo in March 1944 and murdered three months later. It was in the last years of his life, facing the specter of Nazism, that Bloch completed his reflections on the use of history.

The great French historian was manifestly not interested in explaining or seeking sympathy for his own life. Rather, he intended to offer an "apology for history," as the book was titled in French, a defense of the discipline to which he was so passionately dedicated. He emphasized, among other points, that historians must be attentive to the present, as he no doubt was in that dire moment in his life, lest they lapse into a somnolent antiquarianism. What could prevent such a descent was the recognition that history was the study not of what was dead but rather of what was alive. He continued by articulating a pair of key principles that defined the stakes of historical inquiry: "Misunderstanding of the present," he wrote with Santayanan echoes, "is the inevitable consequence of ignorance of the past." At the same time, Bloch observed that "a man may wear himself out just as fruitlessly in seeking to understand the past, if he is totally ignorant of the present."[1]

Bloch insisted on a dialogue between past and present in *The Historian's Craft*. It is only by "borrowing from our daily experiences" that we gain access to the richness and vibrancy of the past. Conversely, he asserted, lines of continuity in structures, forms of reception, and influence extend from the past into the present, providing us with a wide lens onto our current existence.

While *The Historian's Craft* is not an emotionally revealing book, it is hard not to be moved by it—by Bloch's steadfast dedication to his craft, by his sense of the vitality of history, and, not least, by his seeming intuition of the need to produce an epitaph for his labors while in captivity. I often invoked Bloch and his inspiring words in a time of crisis when I welcomed incoming graduate students to the UCLA History Department, where I served as chair for five years. The question these fledgling scholars asked themselves was similar, though of course formulated in a very different, which is to say far less threatening, environment: Why am I committing six years or more of my life to intense and often isolated work with no guarantee of employment upon completion of the Ph.D.?[2]

Especially after the economic crash of 2008, students and their parents have asked this question with ever greater frequency and concern. A drop in student enrollments—at times precipitously, as in the UCLA History Department, which experienced a 40 percent decline from 2007 to 2013—led to a loss of confidence among historians, and humanists in general, about the wisdom of doing what they do. Indeed, there has been abundant talk in recent years of a "crisis of the humanities." The troubles seemed particularly acute at public universities, which do not have the kind of financial cushion that wealthy private institutions do. But even *Harvard Magazine* reported in 2013 on a decline in humanities enrollments at Harvard that prompted that university to establish a task force to address the problem.[3]

This is hardly the first time that the humanities has seemed to be in crisis. In fact, a far more significant decline in enrollments than today's took place in the 1970s, as the literary scholar Michael Bérubé demonstrated in the *Chronicle of Higher Education* in 2013. Bérubé showed that humanities enrollments actually increased in the 1980s and 1990s and that the current numbers "are almost precisely where they were in 1970."[4] His argument adds a healthy dose of historical perspective, reminding us that crises come and go. Indeed, we often assume, while in the midst of a downturn of some sort, that never before in history have such depths been reached. To assuage my own anxieties over the fate of the field of history, I often recall this description of the state of affairs from an eminent scholar: "Student interest in history is waning; the academic job market is contracting. A generation of young Ph.D.'s, having completed their education in a period of scarce financial aid and spiraling costs, are competing for too few tenure-leading jobs, while they face years in short-term, revolving-door appointments. Others, unable to see careers in academe, are retooling and using their skills as historians in journalism, business, government, and organizational work."

This depiction sounds as if it could have been written yesterday. But, in fact, it was expressed thirty-five years ago by the distinguished historian Gerda Lerner when she assumed the presidency of the Organization of American Historians in 1982.[5] Lerner, whom we shall encounter again in the first chapter, offered her assessment in an address called "The Necessity of History." Rather than succumb to the despair of the day, Lerner believed in the therapeutic force of history. History, she declared, "is the means whereby we assert the continuity of human life" through its capacity to shape and form memory.[6] In addition to offering up a notion of history's import, her words remind us that the current generation is not the first nor will it be the last to experience travails of the sort she describes.

Lerner's recollection offers a measure of consolation in ways that history frequently can and has done, as we shall have occasion to explore in Chapter 2. In fact, we already get a clearer picture of history's benefits at this juncture by observing the way it provides depth, perspective, clarity, and solace to the current moment in which we live. Knowing, for example, that the humanities have undergone repeated crises from their inception six hundred years ago in the heart of the Renaissance reassures us that we too can survive the struggles of our day, as well as our own predilection for narratives of decline.[7] This kind of deeper perspective dissolves our myopia and unravels our tightly bound, short-term temporality. Through history, we can position ourselves on a broader temporal landscape with greater accuracy and familiarity, knowing what came before and apprehending what might come after us. In this most serviceable form, history serves as an indispensable bridge not only between past and present, as Marc Bloch affirmed, but between past and future.[8]

THE PERILS AND PROMISE OF THE PAST

The present book is about this serviceable vision of history as it has played out in the modern age. More particularly, it is about the uses to which Jewish history has been put by practitioners of the discipline, most of whom, though by no means all, have been Jews. Akin to peers in other fields, modern Jewish historians have devoted themselves not solely to the task of getting the facts right; they have also sought to draw inspiration, motivation, and clear direction from the past. In doing so, they have often promoted accounts of the past that blur the boundary between history and memory, between the goal of re-creating the past accurately and the task of fortifying pillars of remembrance, which was supposed to be newly reinforced in the modern age. Invoking these terms calls to mind the legacy of Yosef Hayim Yerushalmi (1932–2009), the distinguished historian and author of the now classic *Zakhor* (1982), whose subtitle, "Jewish History and Jewish Memory," marked off opposing poles on a spectrum. Arguing against this dichotomous rendering of the relationship of history to collective memory, and thereby complicating the received understanding of Yerushalmi, I maintain that Jewish historians in the modern age have exemplified the permeability of the border between history and memory in revealing fashion. I further suggest that in the course of their work historians have not only excavated the past but set in place new foundations of memory. They have drawn from historical sources and archives to craft narratives that foster (and in some cases disrupt) the historical recollection of their intended audience. This is one of the key ways in which historians use history to serve the present.

The case of Jewish history presents a clear illustration of the serviceability—and memory-forming features—of history. And yet, these functions are not unique to that case. Today, as in earlier ages, history serves as a vital engine of memory and identity formation for a variety of religious, national, gender, and ethnic groups. Historians frequently make use of the past to advance knowledge or alter misperceptions about groups with which they identify.[9] Eloquent testimony to this mission is offered by John Hope Franklin, the late scholar of African American history. Over the course of six decades, Franklin played a pioneering role in retrieving significant though neglected chapters of U.S. history in which African Americans were central actors, including in his best-known book, *From Slavery to Freedom*, which has sold over three million copies. Franklin understood the importance of disrupting the received narrative of white domination in American history and setting in place a new frame of historical memory, which led him to write not only dozens of monographs but also textbooks intended for school-age children. His work embodied the principle that every new generation of parents aims "to rewrite and reinterpret the nation's history so that their children will be able to understand it better and thus enhance their sense of informed citizenship." He felt an urgent commitment to reinterpret the "nation's history" and expand the bounds of its historical memory as a precondition to social change. On this view, historical knowledge was an essential precondition of social change.[10]

In the complicated universe in which we dwell, there are always risks attending the historian's role as a forger of group memory, especially the distortion and manipulation of evidence. Perhaps the baldest example is Holocaust denial, which stubbornly clings to the claim that millions of Jews were not murdered by the Nazis. Here both ideological fervor and deliberate disregard of a massive trove of evidence seem to be at work.

But the manipulation of evidence in the name of a cause is hardly restricted to this exceptional example. From his distinctive perch, the medievalist Patrick Geary has raised alarm bells about the subservience of modern historical study to the idol of nationalism. This reliance, he writes, "has turned our understanding of the past into a toxic waste dump, filled with the poison of ethnic nationalism, and the poison has seeped deep into popular consciousness."[11]

Geary is joined by the eminent Canadian historian Margaret MacMillan, who sounds a similar warning in *Dangerous Games: The Uses and Abuses of History*, in which she points to the threat of distorting or falsifying history even in the name of a noble ideal. She calls attention to the tendency of ideological partisans to cull evidence selectively to prove "the existence of the nation through time."[12] Trenchant critiques such as these cannot be dismissed lightly. They serve as cautionary notes against the misuse, intentional or not, of the historical medium in framing memory. But they also leave us with an unanswered and perhaps unanswerable question: Where exactly do we draw the line between a surfeit of ideological commitment and acceptable, even unavoidable, political dispositions that no sophisticated practitioner or consumer of history can deny? For example, should we exclude from serious consideration the work of the English historians E. P. Thompson, C. L. R. James, and Eric Hobsbawm because of their unabashed Marxist perspective? These examples suffice to demonstrate that even scholars with deep and visible ideological commitments are capable of illuminating and pathbreaking work.

A second challenge to the utility of history is the fear that historical research is teaching us more and more about less and less. Whereas the concern about ideological distortion relates to the perceived failure of historical scholarship to be objective, the concern about the piling up of historical data goes beyond questions of historical method to the very raison d'être of history. One of the sharpest exponents of this latter issue was Friedrich Nietzsche, whose short essay of 1873–1874, "Vom Nutzen und Nachteil der Historie für das Leben" (On the Advantage and Disadvantage—or Use and Abuse—of History for Life), inspired the subtitle of this book.[13] Nietzsche's essay was written in the wake of an outbreak of chauvinist fervor in Europe that followed the unification of Germany in 1871 and the crushing economic crisis that came shortly thereafter in 1873. In this grim moment, in which his doubts about the forward march of history grew, Nietzsche diagnosed "a malignant historical fever" whose chief symptom was a deluge of historical data that dissolved the holism and integrity of past actors, texts, and events from the past—and thus prevented us from deriving any inspiration from them. The consequences, Nietzsche warned, were dire: "For with a certain excess of history, life crumbles and degenerates, and finally, because of this degeneration, history itself degenerates as well."[14]

Nietzsche's dark admonitions about the excesses of history did not lead him to surrender all hope for history. He catalogued and distinguished among three modes of historical writing: monumental, antiquarian, and critical. Assessing the strengths and weaknesses of each led him to contemplate the prospect of a productive historical enterprise. History *could* serve a valuable educational function, he thought, but only if it operated "in the service of a powerful new life-giving influence."[15] By contrast, if history were pursued for its own sake or only in the name of the false idol of objectivity, it would fail its mission.[16] At times, Nietzsche advocated the path not of remembering but of forgetting the past.

Nietzsche's reflections served as backdrop and inspiration to Yosef Yerushalmi, who also evinced skepticism over the utility of history a century later. Writing in *Zakhor*, Yerushalmi offered this assessment: "The modern effort to reconstruct the Jewish past begins at a time that witnesses a sharp break in the continuity of Jewish living and hence also an ever-growing decay of Jewish group memory. In this sense, if for no other, history becomes what it had never been before—the faith of fallen Jews." Echoing Nietzsche's critique of history for history's sake, Yerushalmi insisted that history "can never substitute for Jewish memory." At best, it might provide a measure of succor or stimulation to those who had experienced the rupture of modernity. The historian, he continued in Nietzschean terms, is not capable of healing the "malady" that results from "the unraveling of that common network of belief and praxis" that undergirds collective memory."[17] Yerushalmi contrasted the modern Jew, who in his opinion suffers from this malady, with the ancient Israelites, who squeezed out of the past a significance that went well beyond the moment. They were "the fathers of meaning in history,"[18] whereas their modern-day heirs swam aimlessly in an ocean of historical details, unable to assign greater or lesser value to any of them. In describing this condition, Yerushalmi recalled Jorge Luis Borges's fictional character Funes the Memorious, who suffers a strange but characteristically modern fate when, after a fall from a horse, he loses the capacity to forget anything.[19] "The shadow of Funes the Memorious," Yerushalmi intoned, "hovers over all of us." The accumulation of historical detail filled Funes's head with "memories" but prevented him from forging a lucid memory upon which to form a coherent sense of the past.[20]

In offering his somewhat dolorous assessment of the state of modern scholarship, Yerushalmi launched a robust discourse about history and memory in the field of Jewish studies and beyond that has lasted to this day.[21] I should add that his words have had particular weight for me, since Yerushalmi was my teacher and mentor at Columbia University. Indeed, it was he who introduced me to the unique challenges and pleasures of studying Jewish history, as he did for so many others.

And yet, I have always sensed that the contrast he posed between history and memory in *Zakhor* was overdrawn.[22] Modern historians are neither completely sequestered in the archive nor altogether detached from the task of memory formation by the rupture of modernity. Indeed, the relationship between history and memory for them is reciprocal. They deploy their professional tools to craft a picture of the past, which can serve—and may well be intended for—those who did not undergo the historical events themselves, but who feel a strong sense of identification with the experiences of their forebears. The resulting picture of the past contributes to forming our memory of the past, which becomes collective when multiple members of a given group are drawn to it. And yet, just as memory is, in this sense, the product, at least in part, of the historian's labors, so too it is a prod to those labors. The nineteenth-century theorist of history Wilhelm Dilthey reminded us that history comes about "thanks to the configuration of its course in memory, which does not reproduce singularity, but reconfigures cohesion itself in its stages."[23] Memory, as a cohesive picture of the past, can be and often has been a platform from which historians commence their inquiry into the past.

When I gave voice to a version of this claim about a reciprocal relationship some fifteen years ago, Yerushalmi sharply and unequivocally disagreed, insisting that modern historians' "reconstructions and interpretations of the Jewish past are most often in open conflict with those preserved in what remains of Jewish collective memory." He expressed strong agreement with the view of his friend, the renowned French scholar Pierre Nora, who declared in the introduction to *Les Lieux de mémoire* that "memory is always suspect in the eyes of history, whose true mission is to demolish it, to repress."[24]

In affirming this divide, Yerushalmi clarified that he was focused on the collective memory associated with traditional Jewish religion and not on "such modern and relatively recent constructs of collective memory as those of Zionism, the Holocaust, or the State of Israel." He further acknowledged that there were tensions between these repositories of memory and "critical historiography."[25] On this point, I am in complete agreement; those kinds of modern memory "constructs," to which historians have undeniably contributed, have been the focus of my attention, both in our exchange and elsewhere.[26] The question remains, however, whether the "traditional" modes of Jewish memory that Yerushalmi sought to differentiate and consign to the past can be so clearly distinguished from the historical memories forged out of movements fueled by modern Jewish national or religious ideologies.

The competing idea that there is an affinity rather than a chasm between history and memory was put forward forcefully in 1989 by Amos Funkenstein, who was one of the few contemporaries in the field who equaled Yerushalmi in erudition and eminence. Responding to *Zakhor* in the newly established journal *History and Memory,* Funkenstein proposed the category of "historical consciousness" as a mediating agent between the poles of history and memory. In contrast to Yerushalmi's depiction of the historian as one who catered to the "faith of fallen Jews," Funkenstein described the historian as a "priest of culture" who tended to the "secular liturgical memory" of the nation-state.[27] He thus offered a very different image of the modern historian from the one Yerushalmi did in *Zakhor,* which went along with his less antagonistic vision of the relationship between history and memory.

But while these two images of the historian differ sharply in both tenor and content, Yerushalmi and Funkenstein may not be entirely irreconcilable. As a number of commentators have already noted, a close examination of key texts in Yerushalmi's oeuvre, including but not restricted to *Zakhor,* yields traces of an alternative view of the function of the historian, one that comes closer to Funkenstein's "priest of culture" than to the image of a scholarly priest ministering to faithless "fallen Jews."[28] Sadly, Yerushalmi is no longer alive to address, affirm, or refute this claim; he passed away in 2009 at the age of seventy-seven. And it is perhaps unfair to project upon him like a ventriloquist a view that he did not clearly articulate. But in the spirit of his own "Monologue with Freud" in *Freud's Moses*,[29] I would like to propose—cognizant of his probable dissent—that Yerushalmi offered up multiple profiles of the modern historian, not simply the one made familiar by *Zakhor*. More than a decade before he published that slender masterwork, in 1970, he devoted a commencement address at Hebrew College in Brookline, Massachusetts, to a reflection on his vocation titled "A Jewish Historian in the 'Age of Aquarius.'" The thirty-eight-year-old Yerushalmi began his speech with a gloss on lyrics from the popular rock musical *Hair,* drawing on its iconic declaration of "the dawning of the Age of Aquarius."[30] He described this "Aquarian" proclamation as reflective of a recurrent apocalyptic sensibility in Jewish and Christian thought: a desire to wipe clean the slate of history. The slogan that captured this sensibility against which Yerushalmi cautioned was: "Down with the past for the sake of the future." Countering the then popular countercultural youth mantra, Yerushalmi asserted that historical amnesia was "not a goal but a disorder." Historians, he added, have an important role to play in healing that disorder. It is they who must ward off the nihilism of Aquarianism by preserving the past; indeed, their first professional obligation is to remember, as in the Hebrew verb *zakhor.* Moreover, it is they, he noted in evocation of the German-American philosopher Eugen Rosenstock-Huessy, who must become "physicians of memory," acting "under a moral pressure to restore a nation's memory, or that of mankind."[31] In this version, the historian is more a traverser of the boundaries of history and memory than a guard standing at a fixed border between them.

Twelve years later, Yerushalmi repeated this quotation from Rosenstock-Huessy in *Zakhor*. But now he cast doubt on the image he had presented to his 1970 audience, arguing that the historian is "at best a pathologist, hardly a physician," more capable of an autopsy than a cure from the past. Our story might plausibly end there, signaling Yerushalmi's mature realization of the limits of history's healing powers. But there is another curious and perhaps countervailing piece of evidence regarding the task of the historian: Yerushalmi's 1993 *Freud's Moses: Judaism Terminable and Interminable,* based on the 1989 Franz Rosenzweig Lectures at Yale University, which was briefly mentioned above.

Confronting the rupture of modernity, Yerushalmi's Freud seeks to move beyond an unbridgeable chasm between history and memory. Yerushalmi attempts to demonstrate this through a detailed reading of Freud's last book, *Moses and Monotheism* (1939). Yerushalmi relates that he was drawn to write *Freud's Moses* as a result of his "profound interest in the various modalities of modern Jewish historicism, of that quest for the meaning of Judaism and Jewish identity through an unprecedented reexamination of the Jewish past which is itself the consequence of a radical break with that past, a phenomenon of which Freud's book is at once an exemplary and idiosyncratic instance."[32] Yerushalmi's inquiry led him to a different summation of Freud's relationship to Judaism from that which previous readers of *Moses and Monotheism* had proposed. Rather than deny the Jews one of their grandest achievements, the development of monotheism, *Moses and Monotheism* revealed Freud's recognition of the Jews' uncommon capacity for survival. In particular, Yerushalmi identified Freud's "psycho-Lamarckism"—his tendency to recognize the ability of Jews to adapt to external circumstances and transmit their evolving sense of collective memory "phylogenetically through the unconscious." Yerushalmi argued that Freud's mission in *Moses and Monotheism* was to expose this lineage, especially its latest irony-bound incarnation, with which he deeply identified: the "fiercely 'godless Jew' who emerges and persists out of what seems to be a final and irreparable rupture in the tradition."[33] The ultimate outcome of Freud's historical labor, which Yerushalmi regarded as an inextricable part of his psychoanalytic project, was the excavation of a unique Jewish type, the Psychological Jew, who somehow persisted as a Jew, albeit "without tradition in any traditional sense."

In crafting this profile, Freud the historian was neither celebrating nor papering over the rupture of the present age. He was both chronicling and living the consequences of it, for indeed it was his personal condition as well. In the "Monologue with Freud" with which he concluded the book, Yerushalmi directly addressed Freud, assuring him (and perhaps himself) that "hardly you alone" dwell in that state.[34] Modern Jews at large were caught in the breach, latter-day heirs of the early modern Marranos, the crypto-Jews who lived outwardly Catholic and inwardly Jewish lives, who interested Yerushalmi throughout his career.[35] So too, he suggested, the modern Jewish chronicler was caught in the breach, but with the added responsibility of explaining this very predicament. In a bold act of self-identification, Yerushalmi recast Freud as a fellow traveler seeking to chart—and to stay afloat in—the swirling byways of Jewish history.

In similar terms, Yerushalmi later recalled with reverence his predecessor in Spanish Jewish history, the German-born Yitzhak (Fritz) Baer, who was the first Jewish historian hired by the new Hebrew University in Jerusalem in 1930. Yerushalmi's introduction to the French edition of Baer's *Galut* in 2000 focused not only on Baer's wide-ranging erudition in Jewish history and the characterization of the German original as a "tour de force" of concision at one hundred pages, but also, and more pointedly, on the fact that it was, like Bloch's, "an extreme book written *in extremis*." Published in 1936, *Galut* summarized, in sweeping and selective fashion, the long history of Jewish thinking about exile. The thinly veiled message of the slim volume in that fateful period, Yerushalmi discerned, was that German Jews "must make every effort to leave the Galut and make their way to the Land of Israel."[36]

Yerushalmi emphasized that his main aim was not to defend Baer but rather to understand him with "humility and a certain respect."[37] Indeed, while he did not share Baer's impulse to negate the Diaspora, he did evince considerable sympathy for "a book not merely by a historian of the Jews, but by a very Jewish historian, existentially implicated in his subject, writing from within Jewish history and addressing his own people in its hour of crisis." He knew well the trying circumstances in which Baer was writing (though they were not yet as dire as those in which Bloch set down his reflections on the historian's craft). Does it strain credulity to suggest that Yerushalmi felt an affinity with Baer, apart from their shared vocation as scholars of Spanish Jewish history? Might he have subconsciously modeled his *Zakhor* on *Galut,* both compact volumes covering vast swaths of history defined by their powerful single Hebrew word titles? Might Baer's volume, and the entire Schocken Bücherei series from which it was drawn, have represented a kind of existentially engaged scholarship that intrigued and inspired Yerushalmi, who was writing in a very different time, though one that induced in him a melancholic sense of loss?[38]

My desire to revisit and complicate Yerushalmi's views stems from more than the autobiographical fact that he was my chief intellectual interlocutor with whom I remain in constant imaginary dialogue. A critical engagement with his views can help us develop a more textured sense of the function of the modern Jewish historian and the broader question of the relationship between history and memory in the modern age. Over the course of Yerushalmi's career, he proposed a variety of models: the Physician of Memory in "The Age of Aquarius," the Fallen Jew of *Zakhor,* the Psychological Jew of *Freud's Moses,* and the "very Jewish historian" writing in extremis in the Baer review.

Each of these personae stood at a distinctive station along a spectrum bounded by the poles of critical history and collective memory. A composite of these types adds up to a profile of the modern Jewish historian as a figure who aspires to bridge the gap between history and memory, mindful of the Sisyphean nature of the task, but not altogether succumbing to despair over it.

This figure is clearly related to, yet distinct from, the melancholic historian of *Zakhor*. That latter figure attested to the profound, and perhaps unbridgeable, rift between history and memory. Indeed, it is not just in *Zakhor* that we see such a stance but in the work of many historians, including Yerushalmi's contemporary (and scholarly foil in matters Freudian) Peter Gay. Gay warned in particularly acute terms against a sort of "lazy and fuzzy thinking" that might lead us to conflate storytelling and critical study of the past. He sharpened the point by observing that "it was not Moses who was the first historian, but Herodotus."[39]

Against this view, in this book I argue that there is ample ground between Moses and Herodotus, between the poles of prophetic storytelling and critical history, as well as between memory and history. Both the earlier and the later Yerushalmi—in contrast to the author of the middle-period *Zakhor*—intuited this, at least as I read him. But even if I am reading him against the grain of his own understanding, , the broader point remains. And it is one which deeply resonates with me. It draws from the insight of the Holocaust historian Saul Friedlander, another of Yerushalmi's intellectual peers, that "an opposition [between history and memory] is far from clear-cut." Friedlander's pioneering work, noteworthy for its simultaneous empirical command and theoretical sophistication, has demonstrated how this opposition can be narrowed when the accumulated results of historical inquiry inform "the prevailing historical consciousness of a group." He points to a middle space between the poles of history and memory in which historians tend to operate, navigating between the quest to describe the past as it was and the impulse to articulate and promote a vision of the past that echoes beyond the archive.[40]

Following in this path, I attempt to examine here the middle space occupied by modern Jewish historians as they mediate between the poles of history and memory. I believe that this middle space not only merits attention; it should be recognized as fertile ground on which to construct a vision of the utility of history—not as a begrudging concession to an inescapable subjectivity but as a realization of its power and efficacy to serve society in multiple ways.[41] Indeed, it is in this middle space that I dwell as a historian.

A ROADMAP: BETWEEN HISTORY AND MEMORY

This book comes in the midst of or perhaps at the end of a robust discussion over the relationship between history and memory that has taken place over the past few decades.[42] Many intellectual sources inspired this discourse, including representatives of the French *Annales* School (Fernand Braudel, Pierre Nora, Mona Ozouf, and François Furet), German cultural memory studies (Aleida Assmann and Jan Assmann), and Holocaust-related research (Friedlander, Lawrence Langer, Dominick LaCapra, and James Young). An important early inspiration was the French sociologist Maurice Halbwachs, who analyzed in *La Mémoire collective* (1950) the social frameworks that enable and contain a group's memory. Yosef Yerushalmi himself drew from Halbwachs at the outset of *Zakhor,* in which he identified ritual, liturgy, and commemorative acts as part of the rich fabric of group memory.[43] The fourth chapter, however, marked a shift in focus from collective memory to the function and intentions of the modern historian.

While much scholarly attention on memory has been trained on the recollections, remembrances, and ritual practices of groups, my interest in this book is on the latter and narrower understanding of memory as the product of the individual historian's constructive and constitutive act. This interest rests, in turn, on an understanding of the work of the historian that borrows from the mid-twentieth-century philosopher R. G. Collingwood. Collingwood, as I elaborate in a brief methodological postscript, grasped the historian's labor as a concerted mental effort aimed at "re-enactment," a process of the historian's "re-thinking for himself the thought of his author."[44]

In the process of re-enactment, historians bring parts of themselves, in all their variegated humanness, into the interpretive process. They shape images of the past not through unmediated access to raw historical data but through a process of mental imagination that mixes a careful sifting of sources and a healthy measure of cognitive creativity. This combination of functions allows the historian to piece together shards of historical evidence into a coherent narrative formation. At times, that narrative formation undergirds the collective memory of a group with which the historian identifies. At other times, the historian proceeds with the conscious intention to disrupt, upend, or replace older memory formations with new ones.

This sort of work, it bears repeating, is not unique to Jewish historians. Scholars in other fields have repeatedly used their professional tools to revise or discard existing historical narratives that they regard as partial in the name of a more accurate or serviceable one. It also bears noting that one need not be a member of a particular group to engage in historically informed political activism or the work of memory formation related to it. In the case of Jewish historical scholarship, whose modern practitioners have been overwhelmingly Jewish until now, more and more scholars today come with little Jewish background or are not Jews.[45] Some, perhaps most, approach the field as a subject of pure scholarly interest, no more nor less. Others approach it, however, with more utilitarian or instrumental aims.

An example worth considering is contemporary Germany, where non-Jews predominate in the various Jewish studies programs that stretch from Munich to Hamburg. Whereas before the Holocaust, Wissenschaft des Judentums was primarily populated by Jews, the postwar work of Jewish studies in Germany is overwhelmingly, and understandably, run by non-Jews.[46] From its inception, the postwar project of Jewish studies was part of a larger, difficult process by which Germany confronted its criminal past, known in German as *Vergangenheitsbewältigung*. This process picked up particular momentum in the 1980s, as a fierce debate among historians about the singularity of Germany's crimes known as the *Historikerstreit* entered the public domain.[47] Through this charged debate, the past became vividly, even explosively, alive in the present—in public discourse, in educational settings, in literary circles. In parallel, the intense focus on the place of Nazism and the Holocaust in the German past added new relevance and meaning to Jewish studies.[48] Faculty and students increasingly engaged topics of contemporary relevance such as German-Jewish history, the Holocaust and antisemitism, and Zionism and the State of Israel. They did so for a variety of reasons: to answer deeply existential questions about their own (or their parents') identity, out of a sense of moral obligation to the victims of Nazism, and as a way of restoring memory of a vibrant Jewish cultural presence to the German landscape.[49]

This example suggests that existential engagement and a personal connection to the study of the Jewish past are not exclusive to Jews. Jewish historians of various stripes and religions have used the study of the past not only for the declared purpose of pure research but also for an array of political, ethical, and personal aims. In doing so, they have exemplified some of the manifold utilities of history and pointed to the will of the historian not just to record but to shape our picture of the past.

It is my mission in the present book to uncover that will and excavate its myriad effects in the work of modern historians. To those familiar with the history of Jewish historical writing, some of the terrain covered will be recognizable. What is distinctive is that each of the three main chapters follows a guiding theme that has prompted the modern Jewish historian to traverse the porous boundary between history and memory. The three themes—liberation, consolation, and witness—are hardly exhaustive. Historians, after all, have been guided in their work by many different motifs and motives. But these themes are not random either. They rise to the surface after a sustained reading of modern Jewish historical scholarship, revealing the often unwitting fealty of its practitioners to religiously inspired themes that are deeply rooted in their cultural backgrounds. This fealty, in turn, points to continuities in theme and function between medieval chroniclers and modern historians.

Relying on this link, I imagine this book as a lesser, albeit more directed and applied version of what Marc Bloch called his "apologie pour l'histoire." Thus, I set out in the conclusion my own sense of the link between past and present, arguing for the importance of history as an ingredient in informed civic debate. Throughout, I seek to push beyond the fashionably flip dismissal of "identity politics" by suggesting that the historian's emotional and identitarian investments are neither avoidable nor wholly negative: they can open new horizons of research and insert a note of urgency and relevance into the scholarly undertaking.[50] This is not, for me, an abstract matter. My own Jewish and political commitments have guided my historical explorations of the relationship between history and memory, as well as my ongoing interest in the relationship between Jews and Arabs in Israel/Palestine. Concomitantly, I believe that historical research, informed by passion *and* judiciousness, can be a productive resource both in fortifying and helpfully disrupting memory, as well as in exposing us to the human face of our seeming enemy.

In this way, I attempt to bridge the ways in which Jewish historians have functioned in the past and the ways in which history and historians might function today. At one level, the sheer volume of historical data, made ever more plentiful in our internet age, is so overwhelming as to make some amount of forgetting a necessity, if not an actual desideratum. And yet, we do so at our own collective risk, for historical knowledge amplifies our ability to understand the world in which we live and which we hope to pass on to future generations. So too the strands of memory that historians weave together make comprehensible the worlds we live in, often in enriching ways, though also at times in excessively particularistic ways that induce fear of the "other." Therein lies the potential for abuse in history. Notwithstanding that danger, and despite the gravitational pull toward forgetting in our twenty-first-century state of information overload, we would do well to acknowledge and avail ourselves of historical knowledge as a useful implement in the toolkit of societal repair.

History as Liberation

We begin our profile of the task of the Jewish historian in the modern age with an important, if at some level counterintuitive, goal: history as liberation. On the face of it, and at the most latent level, history is about the past. Historians use an array of sources and methods to immerse themselves in it. Leopold von Ranke, the nineteenth-century Prussian historian, notably, though not uncontroversially, expressed the belief that the historian should "extinguish" himself in order to gain access to the past.[1]

The attempt to understand and even enter the past would seem to be a necessarily preservative act. In fact, historians relish the prospect of settling into an archive and being transported back to a world which they happily and painstakingly reconstruct. But this impulse toward reconstruction is but one facet of the historian's vocation. We need only recall the specter of presentism of which historians have periodically accused one another—that is, the tendency to read, and even bend, the past through the lens of the current moment. This impulse is misguided, critics say, because history "is not a redeemer, promising to solve all human problems in time." Indeed, its focus, Arthur Schlesinger, Jr., once observed, is "anxiety and frustration, not progress and fulfillment."[2]

But mustn't we ask, Are we not all, at some level, presentists, as even Herbert Butterfield, the author (and erstwhile critic) of *The Whig Interpretation of History,* came to realize?[3] Not only are historians undeniably products of their time and place, but they have consistently applied the results of their research to present and future concerns—wittingly and unwittingly. Indeed, we have been extracting meaning, guidance, and direction from the past for as long as we have been recording it. And at times, we summon up the past in order to liberate or be liberated. The political theorist Michael Walzer has chronicled how the repeated invocation of the biblical story of Exodus served, in a wide variety of times and settings, as inspiration for movements of liberation. In many of the cases he observed in *Exodus and Revolution,* a persistent companion of the theme of liberation was religion, natural enough given the centrality of the Exodus story in the Jewish, Christian, and Islamic traditions.[4]

To our modern, secular minds, the relationship between religion and liberation seems oppositional rather than complementary. Religion often appears to be a conservative, even reactionary, force. And in fact, we will explore in this chapter how numerous modern scholars imagined history as a medium to liberate themselves and others from ossified forms of Jewish religion. But we shall also take stock of the obverse—a number of cases in which history has been utilized as a force of liberation *on behalf of* religion.

There are, of course, multiple catalysts for historiographical liberation. And thus, we will move from our initial discussion of religion to consider other instances in which history was mobilized to the task of liberation: for example, when history was called on to promote national liberation or women's liberation. This will afford us the opportunity not only to reread the course of modern Jewish historiography, a story that has been told more than a few times. It will also allow us to explore the motif of liberation through the lens of its political utility, in the expansive sense of promoting a goal that extends beyond the realm of scholarship itself.

To gain a sense of what this kind of mobilization looks like, we recall two prominent American historians of recent years. While neither was a specialist in Jewish history, both came from distinctive Jewish backgrounds that played a consequential role in their formations: Gerda Lerner and Howard Zinn. Lerner was born in Vienna, from which she took flight just before Kristallnacht, coming to the United States alone at age nineteen; Zinn was born to a poor immigrant family in Brooklyn. Coming of intellectual age in the charged environment of New York in the thirties and forties, the two followed a familiar Jewish path by embracing Marxism as young adults before turning away from it later in life. Throughout they remained unwavering in their commitment to social justice—and more to the point, to the use of history as a key agent of change. Lerner, who titled an autobiographical volume *Living with History/Making Social Change,* utilized her professional training to overcome the exclusion or marginalization of women from received accounts of the past, and in the process to become one of this country's pioneers of women's history. Zinn, for his part, combined huge scholarly and political passions to rewrite the history of the United States by focusing on the forgotten voices—Native Americans, slaves, unionists, and others. His labors, most significantly in *A People's History of the United States* (1980), won him a wide audience, ample praise, and fierce denunciation for subjecting history to his ideological precepts.[5] We could easily find fault with Zinn's predictability and a priori preferences, but we ignore his insistence on listening to the voices of the suppressed at considerable risk.

These two scholars do not represent, to be sure, all historians.[6] But they do stand as exemplars of the urgency of history, as well as of the way history has been used as a tool of liberation. The two manifested in their work a powerful tendency to recover and reveal, "by exposing," as Zinn put it, "those facts that any society tends to hide about itself."[7] At the same time, there is in their work, and in the work of many others, an impulse to study the past precisely in order to be freed from it. This principle allows us to propose an addendum to George Santayana's famous aphorism that "those who cannot remember the past are condemned to repeat it." That is, those who *can* remember the past are perhaps best able to move beyond it. Far from being a rare occurrence, this has been a guiding principle for historians, particularly for modern Jewish historians, as we shall now examine in closer detail.

FROM PROTESTANT POLEMICS TO ORTHODOX APOLOGETICS

Our story begins with the first major chronicler of the Jews in the modern age, Jacques Basnage, the early-eighteenth-century French Huguenot scholar who wrote the first major postbiblical history of the Jews, beginning with a six-volume version in French (1706–7) and concluding with a fifteen-volume edition in Dutch (1716).[8] Basnage took flight from his native France for the Netherlands in search of religious freedom for Protestants. He saw himself as picking up the account where the first-century C.E. historian Flavius Josephus had left off more than sixteen centuries earlier. Akin to Josephus, who chronicled the devastating military defeat of his own people, Basnage fashioned himself as a scholar who transcended partisanship—and especially the narrow perspective of the rabbis, who, he lamented, "are but little acquainted with their History."[9] At the same time, he was fueled by a missionary zeal and polemical energy born of his day. Thus, he was desirous of proving, in tones reminiscent of Spinoza some three decades earlier, that the election of the Jews was time bound and that, in their postbiblical life, they "had nothing remarkable to distinguish themselves from other Nations."[10] On the contrary, their many dispersions stood as territorial evidence of a basic theological claim: namely, that "the present Calamity of the *Jews* is enough to convince us, that

God is exasperated against them, and that their Sins deserve that Blindness, which made God reject them." And yet, his history would have been far shorter were Basnage not committed to revealing the kind of meticulous detail—and not just of the biblical text—that one might expect of an incipient modern historian (without access to archival sources). It might also have been shorter had Basnage not sought to disparage living Jews by associating them with a group he reviled even more, Catholics, whom he held responsible for his own departure from France. What becomes clear is that the rationale for this expansive history lay not in Basnage's intrinsic interest in the history of the Jews. The aim, he explained, was unmistakable: "We ought to have a clearer Knowledge of a Nation, to whom we have succeeded, and that shall be one day united with the Christian Church."[11] In other words, he wrote his history of the Jews as a means of demonstrating that Christianity had superseded Judaism and thus could liberate Christians—and, he hoped, Jews as well—from the ignominious Jewish past of theological error, ritual excess, and moral corruption to a state of salvation.

A similar impulse guided a chronicler of the Jews a century later in the newly established United States, the intrepid amateur scholar of religion Hannah Adams. Operating in a Protestant New England ambience permeated with intense interest in the Old Testament, Hebrew, and the Jews, Adams wrote her two-volume *History of the Jews from the Destruction of Jerusalem to the Present Time* (1812), which drew heavily on Basnage. While evincing sympathy for the Jews and "the calamities they have endured," she betrayed clear traces of a good Christian intent on the conversion of the Jews. Their history "exhibits a melancholy picture of human wretchedness and depravity," which she then catalogued: "the wild fury of fanaticism, the stern cruelty of avarice, a succession of massacres; a repetition of plunders, shades without light; [and] a dreary wilderness, unenlivened with one spot of verdure."[12] Chronicling this tale of woe, though, had a clear benefit, Adams continued:

> The exemption of the Jews from the common fate of nations, affords a striking proof of the truth of the sacred scriptures. They are, as was foretold, dispersed over the habitable globe, being themselves the depositories of those oracles in which their own unbelief and consequent suffering are clearly predicted. . . . One of the great designs of their being preserved and continued a distinct people appears to be, that their singular destiny might confirm the divine authority of the Gospel, which they reject; and that they might strengthen the faith of others in those sacred truths, to which they refuse to yield their own assent.[13]

Adams, like Basnage before her, regarded the history of the Jews as affirmation of the truth of Christianity. In this regard, her work was continuous with a long series of Christian polemicists. And yet, unlike those Christians who preceded her, she conveyed her supersessionism in a highly detailed, footnoted historical narrative in which she "spared no exertions in her power to collect authentic documents."[14] This impulse, along with an interest in the present-day story of the Jews shared by Basnage, offered up a novel template for the study of Jewish history. It entailed fealty to the emerging standards of the modern historical discipline, as well as a clear commitment to utilize history to illumine the path of liberation from the shackles of the past.

The first modern *Jewish* historical researchers also subscribed to this set of disciplinary norms and sense of purpose, albeit with different views of the liberatory power of history. One of the pioneering figures of Wissenschaft des Judentums, Leopold Zunz, made this abundantly clear in his bold programmatic essay "Etwas über die rabbinische Literatur" (On Rabbinic Literature), published six years after Adams's book. The twenty-three-year-old Zunz surveyed the decrepit state of Jewish studies in 1818 with preternatural wisdom and maturity. "Unsere Wissenschaft," as he termed it—"our science"—had come, like Hegel's Owl of Minerva, to take stock of a wide body of postbiblical Jewish literature out of which "no new significant development" was to be expected.[15] In fact, Zunz notably, though inaccurately, predicted that "Hebrew books are more readily available than they will likely be in 1919." At the same time, he believed that a serious assessment of the breadth and depth of postbiblical literature must overcome the stranglehold of modern Christian scholars, who distorted the visage of Judaism for their own religious purposes. Motivated by a desire to disparage rather than respect, they tended to regard anything that "can be used against the Jews or Judaism . . . [as] a welcome find."[16]

At this point, we encounter a seeming paradox. *History*, or at least a scholarly perspective deeply informed by history, was being called upon to liberate the study of Jewish sources from *history*—namely, a history laden by Christian bias. Indeed, history served not only as a series of events and a narrative account of those events but as a liberatory and an oppressive force. This Janus-faced quality opened history up to various angles of criticism, which gained momentum in the nineteenth century.[17] But it also pointed to a new public utility—and urgency—for historically based scholarship such as Wissenschaft des Judentums. Leopold Zunz understood this well when he declared in 1845 that "the equal status of the Jews in ethics and life will emerge with the equal status of the Wissenschaft des Judentums." That is, when the day arrived that the study of Jewish religion and history was validated through recognition as a legitimate field in the university, then it would both enable and be a short path to the recognition of Jews as worthy members of European and German society.[18]

Meanwhile, the spirit of historical scholarship as liberation animated not only the younger generation of Jewish intellectuals of which Zunz was an exemplar but a more elderly Bohemian Jew by the name of Peter Beer who lived in Prague.[19] A few years after Zunz produced his programmatic essay, Beer published another contribution to a long row of works that he had written about Jewish history. Distinct from his previous surveys in Hebrew, this new two-volume German study, published in 1822–1823, was devoted to a very particular theme: Jewish sectarian movements throughout the ages. Beer laid claim to the spirit of nonpartisanship that historians of his generation were proudly announcing. The goal of the self-respecting historian, he announced at the outset, was to present the past without celebrating or distorting it. At the same time, the value of studying the past rested on its ability to provide guidance for the present.

Beer proved more adept at the latter task than the former— that is, at using history to provide guidance for the present than at avoiding his own clear bias. Although he was hardly a lover of some of the sectarian movements he studied—he had particular disdain for Hasidism—he nonetheless elaborated on their history and doctrines in order to challenge the hegemony of *Rabbinismus*, "rabbinism," as normative Judaism. His account of the various "sects" he studied, tendentious as it was, was designed to topple rabbinism from its primacy within Judaism, to be replaced by what Beer called "pure Mosaism."[20] What exactly was that?

"Pure Mosaism," according to Beer, was primal Judaism stripped of the layers of interpretive and ritual accretion that rabbis had placed on the biblical foundation. Beer's notion of a pristine Judaism readily calls to mind the sixteenth-century Portuguese *converso* turned Jew turned heretic Uriel da Costa, who inveighed against the "Pharisees" of his day in order to reveal a deeply submerged Mosaism.

Whereas da Costa used the language of religious polemics, familiar to him from Portugal and Amsterdam, to wage his battle, Beer prosecuted his case in a nineteenth-century idiom, history, which was endowed with a distinctly utilitarian function. Both, however, were animated by the same goal of liberation from the crushing burden of rabbinic authority. Both were mindful of past examples of attempted liberators, especially the medieval Karaites, with whom Beer in particular identified.[21]

Karaism was, as many have observed (beginning with Richard Simon in the seventeenth century), a sort of Protestantism *avant la lettre*, sharing with the later and more powerful movement a commitment to bore through the bedrock of clerical obfuscation to the ancient font of scriptural faith.[22] The association here is not accidental. Although Peter Beer was raised in Catholic Prague, his interest in Karaism reflects a Protestant theological and historicist arc that covered much of central Europe in the nineteenth century.[23] That is, his impulse to use history to chisel away at rabbinic ossification was, in a sense, a Protestant move. And it was hardly unique to him. He was preceded by Jacques Basnage and Hannah Adams, and he was followed by a number of nineteenth-century Jewish scholars intent on liberating a long suppressed and pure version of their religion.

One thinks in this context of the greatest of German Reform rabbis and scholars in the nineteenth century, Abraham Geiger. Scholars have long noted that Geiger consciously swam against the current of Protestant scholarship in his day; among the more recent, Susannah Heschel argues that his main motive was not to Christianize Judaism but rather, in a precocious postcolonial move, to Judaize Christianity (and particularly Christ).[24] To be sure, that was a key part of Geiger's mission. But we must also recall his deep sense of malaise, especially as a young man, over Judaism's condition. His letters to his friend, the Franco-

German scholar Joseph Derenbourg, abound with references to Judaism as ossified, fossilized, and diseased. Geiger confided to Derenbourg in 1841 that he lacked faith that "a truly living force . . . may yet well up from Judaism."[25] If hope *were* to be found for some form of revival, it might issue from a historically grounded Wissenschaft. For that scholarly force, Geiger asserted, "is the sum total of the entire intellectual development of mankind, constantly striving for *liberation* from the limiting one-sided effects of transitory and strictly national phenomena."[26] History was the methodological tool to record, register, and, in some sense, promote that liberation. Geiger found a good model in his day in David Friedrich Strauss's pathbreaking and controversial book of 1835, *Das Leben Jesu* (The Life of Jesus), whose searching and provocative nature was "of sufficient significance to be used as a source of support."[27]

Interestingly, Geiger drew methodological inspiration and a measure of courage from Strauss in offering up his own *un-Protestant* view of Jesus as a Jew. At the same time, there were more than glimmers of a *Protestant* narrative arc in his thought. We gain a glimpse of this in the lectures that Geiger delivered as a kind of career summation between 1872 and 1874 as a professor at the newly created rabbinical seminary in Berlin, the Hochschule für die Wissenschaft des Judentums. There, Geiger laid out a sweeping periodization of the evolution of Judaism that focused on four stages. The first three were Revelation, an age of "vigorous creation"; Tradition, in which "biblical material was processed, shaped and molded for life"; and Legalism, marked by "toilsome preoccupation with the heritage" and casuistry. Of the last period, Geiger wrote: "The fourth period, the era of *liberation* has been marked by an effort to loosen the fetters of the previous era *by means of the use of reason and historical research*. However, the bond with the past has not been severed. What is being attempted is solely to revitalize Judaism and to cause the stream of history to flow forth once again. This is the era of *Critical Study,* our own modern era."[28]

The aim of Geiger's periodization scheme was twofold: first, to reconnect contemporary Judaism to the living current of its glorious past, from which it had been severed; and second, to do so by adopting a dynamic view of historical development to be liberated from a burdensome past, especially from the age of "rigid legalism," which was marked by "petrification" and "paralysis of thought" in *Jewish* culture (through active engagement by Jews with the broader host society).[29] The coexistence of moribund and vibrant cultural forces, even in the same period, points to the dialectical view of history that Geiger favored. According to his expansive historicist vision, "every development is possible only within the framework of history."[30] And as he clarified, later developments were "already inherent in the growth and flowering process of the original seeds." Wissenschaft's liberatory role, then, was to retrieve the original seeds by clearing away the crowded undergrowth, revealing what was still vibrant in Judaism.[31]

This vision of history, which was intended to reshape the way Jews remembered the past, went hand in hand with Geiger's project to reform Judaism. He and other nineteenth-century religious reformers sought to discard that which was moribund in favor of what was still vital. They applied their historical research directly to the battles they were waging within the German-Jewish community over whether it was permissible to make changes to Jewish liturgy and ritual. Geiger, for example, played a prominent role at the second conference of reform rabbis in 1845, advocating for the use of German in prayer since Hebrew "has ceased to be alive for the people" and "a German prayer strikes a deeper chord than a Hebrew prayer."[32]

But it was not only Geiger and his liberal colleagues who availed themselves of historical tools in order to revive, rehabilitate, or liberate memory of the past. Jews at the other end of the emerging denominational spectrum in the nineteenth century also made use of history for their own liberatory purposes, though a bit later in the century. We know of the work of Wissenschaft scholars of the Orthodox persuasion such as Jakob Barth, Abraham Berliner, and David Zvi Hoffmann, who introduced historical methods to their students at the Orthodox seminary founded by Rabbi Esriel Hildesheimer in 1873 in Berlin. More recently, scholars have devoted new attention to the largely neglected substratum of writing called Orthodox or Haredi historiography issuing largely from eastern Europe.[33]

In this body of work, we can see the other side of the coin of the liberating effects of history with respect to religion—that is, liberation from the deleterious effects of secularism. I would like to illustrate this tendency by focusing on two exemplars, separated by a century or so but joined in their commitment to free the past from the biases of secular historians. The first is Zeev Jawitz, the least recognizable of an august and well-known group of Jewish scholars from the nineteenth and twentieth centuries: the authors of major, multivolume histories of the Jews, of whom we think principally of Heinrich Graetz, Simon Dubnow, and Salo W. Baron.

Far less known, Jawitz, a Polish-born Orthodox scholar and Zionist, wrote a fourteen-volume history of the Jews called *Toldot Yisra'el* (History of Israel). Grounded in traditional rabbinic reverence and learning, Jawitz also read widely in modern scholarship, which provided him with the confidence to address a deficiency that troubled him. On the face of it, the problem was simple: "Most Gentile scholars of Jewish history and thought distort it or are deficient, to a lesser or greater extent, both in terms of their knowledge base and their biases, which prevent them from accumulating adequate knowledge of the Jews."[34]

But in fact, the problem was deeper than Gentile bias. Many notable Jewish scholars of Jewish history in Germany had fallen under the sway of Gentile contemporaries in writing the history of their own people. Jawitz lamented in eerily prescient language in 1895 that they "were unable to liberate themselves from the burden of the teachings of their Aryan professors." He sought to undertake a corrective. In the first instance, he wrote his volumes not in German, the dominant language of modern Jewish scholarship to that point, but in Hebrew, which was in the early stages of development as a modern scholarly language. His use of Hebrew reflected a more intimate and unabashed connection to his historical objects than the German used by his colleagues. In fact, his history was extraordinarily deferential to the chronology and sources of traditional rabbinic Judaism, with a majority of his volumes (nine of fourteen) treating the biblical and Talmudic periods. Animating his work was the desire to reclaim the history of his people from subservient, largely German Jewish, scholars. In an ironic echo of Heinrich Graetz's brash assertion to Leopold Zunz, Jawitz made clear that he was not seeking to replicate the old tendencies of Wissenschaft des Judentums but rather intended to write "a Jewish history that revealed an inner richness like no other, that would be a fount of life that would never lead astray."[35]

Jawitz's work did not reach a wide audience with his first volumes. On one hand, a series of negative reviews from scholars such as Simon Dubnow and Yosef Klausner probably turned away the growing audience of secular Hebrew readers in eastern Europe. On the other, the appetite among Orthodox Jews for a history of the Jews in Hebrew was not especially deep at the fin de siècle. As a result, the book, as the historian Michael Brenner has noted, fell between the cracks of religious traditionalism and secular Zionism.[36]

Notwithstanding this predicament, Jawitz's series had gone

through five editions by the 1950s, suggesting that history was gaining traction as a genre worth reading for Orthodox Jews. And since that time there has been an appreciable increase in works of history and biography in Hebrew, Yiddish, and English intended specifically for an Orthodox audience. Perhaps most illustrative of this trend is the popularity of the ArtScroll imprint of the Mesorah Publishing Company in Brooklyn, New York, which since 1975 has published a wide array of books intended for a traditionally observant clientele, especially easily accessible versions of sacred texts (such as the Bible and the Talmud) in English translation. ArtScroll also puts out a range of books on food, psychology, and history, which share the goal with the reproduced holy works of upending "inadequate, distorted, or otherwise illegitimate representations of Jewish knowledge, ritual practice, and historical imagination" and replacing them with "corrected, more authentic, more reliable, and better organized" versions.[37]

One of the most prolific authors in the ArtScroll stable is the second Orthodox exemplar, the Israeli-American writer Rabbi Berel Wein. Rabbi Wein has produced a vast corpus of work in multiple fields. He is especially known as the author of biographical and historical books that present a traditional Orthodox rendering notable for its reverential quality, especially his four-volume history of the Jews that extends from antiquity to 1990. Although he was writing a century after Zeev Jawitz, Rabbi Wein shared the impulse to use a particular kind of historical narrative to free readers from what both regarded as the dangerous hold of secularism. Wein made this clear in his five-hundred-page modern Jewish history *The Triumph of Survival*, which he opened by insisting that "history is too important to be left to the historians," all the more so when it is a matter of Jewish history. Insofar as previous accounts have been "almost exclusively the product of secular Jews," it was time to reclaim the past. To do so required a profession of faith that is foreign to most professional historians today, though far less uncommon in the age of Ranke.[38] Wein declared, "I am an Orthodox Jew who believes in the divinity of Jewish tradition and in the uniqueness of the people of Israel." He continued by admitting that "there is an Author and Planner, Who guides Israel to its destiny." Interestingly, Wein had absorbed enough of the ethos of the modern historian to aver that one must "accept truth from whoever says it," whether it comes from Jewish sources or no. And yet, the goal was unmistakable: it was to write, in the tradition of Graetz and Jawitz, not just another history of the Jews but an unapologetically *Jewish* history.[39] This meant liberating Jewish history from the assimilatory biases of modern Jewish historiography, including those of Graetz himself. No longer, for example, was Moses Mendelssohn, the late-eighteenth-century German-Jewish philosopher, considered—even by prominent Orthodox figures such as S. R. Hirsch and Jawitz—the great hero who revitalized Jewish life and culture.[40] On Wein's reading, Mendelssohn, notwithstanding his commitment to Jewish ritual observance, "loosed forces that would be destructive to myriads of Jews individually and to the Jewish people as a whole." His philosophy was but "a reflection of the incipient disaster that he was so prominent in fashioning."[41]

Wein's self-described "traditional Jewish perspective of history" sought to reorient the lens onto the past toward a narrative that was affirming, not corrosive, of religious faith. Like Jawitz, he aimed to craft a reverential collective memory, albeit in an uncommon medium, history. Wein's use of history, and his goal to herald "the triumph of survival," is its own form of assimilation to a modern mode of thought even though it was intended to safeguard against its most deleterious effects. This "assimilation" raises the question of how Wein's form of historiographical liberation differs from or resembles that of contemporary professional scholars from whom he seeks a measure of distance. In his recent history of Jewish historiography, Michael Brenner compares Wein to the renowned Berkeley rabbinicist Daniel Boyarin on the basis of their shared willingness to identify with the objects of their research, as well as to acknowledge heroes and villains in their accounts.[42] This is an interesting comparison, but it should not obscure the fact that not all forms of historiographical liberation—nor all identitarian projects—are identical. Boyarin's balance of aims and practices is different from Wein's, and the two write different kinds of books, one marked by cutting-edge theoretical insights, critical apparatus, and radical politics, and the other by an unadorned storyline without any gesture to theory or the professional scholarly guild that aims to convey unquestioned fealty to traditional rabbinic authority. The two not only appeal to vastly different audiences; they mix scholarly and ideological proclivities in different balances. We thus can speak of a spectrum along which historians and other scholarly writers dwell, with one pole marking out the criterion of sharp criticism and the other unalloyed reverence.

FROM EMANCIPATION TO AUTO-EMANCIPATION

Up to this point, we have focused on a range of authors from Jacques Basnage to Berel Wein who believed that history not only emancipates from the shackles of past bias but pushes toward a new form of religious enlightenment. History can also be and has been mobilized for other kinds of liberations, including release from ignorance, bias, and discrimination. Whereas some seek epistemological clarity, others seek a measure of political freedom through study of the past.[43] One of the clearest cases among modern Jewish scholars was one of the earliest: Leopold Zunz, whom we remember as a founding father of Wissenschaft des Judentums. Born in 1794, Zunz was a child of the

French Revolution and remained throughout his life fired with enthusiasm for the ideals of liberty, equality, and fraternity. He brought these values to bear on a number of influential studies of the 1830s, which represented examples of what we might call "applied history." For instance, Zunz declared in a hard-hitting introduction to his 1832 history of the sermon (excised by Prussian censors in the first edition) that "it is finally time that Jews in Europe, especially in Germany, be granted the Right and Freedom, not rights and freedoms." An important way forward was to examine the past in order to illuminate and liberate it from darkness. In the case of this particular book, Zunz sought to show not only the edificatory value of the sermonic form in general but that Jews had used this form throughout their history, frequently in the vernacular tongue of the day. He thus argued strenuously against the effort by the conservative Friedrich Wilhelm III, king of Prussia, to ban Jewish sermonizing in German. The ultimate goal was to uproot "clericalism and inquisition, despotism and slavery, torture and censorship" in favor of "Freedom, Wissenschaft, and Civilization."[44]

Zunz's commitment to use historical scholarship to promote Jewish political rights continued in his 1837 study, *Namen der Juden: Eine geschictliche Untersuchung* (Names of the Jews: A Historical Investigation). Here, too, Zunz sought to battle the forces of reaction in Prussia that sought to limit Jews to biblical names so as to ensure their ongoing segregation. His historical brief argued that Jews had been adopting non-Jewish names for millennia, extending back to the Babylonian exile in the sixth century B.C.E., and thus should be permitted to continue this practice.[45]

Zunz sought to maximize the potential of history to effect change in the present age, whose conservative character he saw as a sign of messianic birth pangs. To be sure, his efforts were not limited to research. He became a fervent political activist in the 1840s, marching, demonstrating, and agitating—all in the belief that the "bloody Day of Judgment is at hand for the oppressors of so many nations."[46] So too, he was convinced, was the age of emancipation.

The oft-invoked image of the cloistered and disengaged scholar held little water in this period, with reference to neither Zunz nor to his contemporaries. The twentieth-century historian Salo W. Baron undertook a wide-ranging survey of the involvement of Jewish studies scholars in the struggle for emancipation in 1848 in Europe and concluded that "the accusation frequently leveled against the science of Judaism that it had isolated itself from the mainstream of Jewish life and, hence, tended to become petrified had no foundations at all during the Revolutionary period, and for many years thereafter." Indeed, scholars in Prussia, France, Italy, Austria, Bohemia, Moravia, Hungary, Galicia, and even the United States—a veritable *Who's Who* of Jewish studies in mid-century—readily joined in the springtime revolutionary fervor.[47]

In that era, history was mobilized to the task of *emancipation*, reflecting the quest of Jews for full civic rights in Europe. A half-century later, history was mobilized to the task of *auto-emancipation*, the phrase made famous by the Russian-Jewish doctor Leon Pinsker in his 1882 pamphlet of that name.[48] No longer content to rely on the beneficence of Gentile hosts in Europe, Pinsker and those who followed in his wake sought to transform the Jews from a collection of enlightened individuals into a proud and self-sustaining nation. This early generation of Jewish nationalists established an oft-repeated pattern by making recourse to history as a tool of liberation.

Perhaps most significant in this regard was the prototypical Jewish nationalist historian Simon Dubnow, who will make frequent appearances in the remainder of this book. Dubnow was equally well known for his comprehensive historical purview, spanning the entirety of the Jewish past, and his commitment as a leading advocate of diaspora nationalism. At the outset of his career, Dubnow crafted a sweeping vision for the role of Jewish history, initially published in Russian in 1891 and then in revised form a year later in Hebrew.[49] The essay's title—"Let Us Seek and Investigate"—reveals its programmatic qualities, akin in scale and ambition to the manifesto produced seventy-four years earlier by Leopold Zunz. Dubnow combined in the essay a set of philosophical reflections, principles of periodization, and research objectives. He started off by averring that one of the three main sources of Jewish unity was the sense of a shared historical destiny. And yet Jews over the ages were surprisingly bad at committing their history to written records. "Why is it," Dubnow asked, that "knights of the Torah . . . have left us thousands of responsa, books of casuistry, collections of laws, commentaries on the Bible and its exegetes as well as scientific and philosophical studies, and yet have not bequeathed us an historical literature?" Longingly, Dubnow held that those who sought to reverse this neglect in the modern age—indeed, who understood history's "great value for the future of our people"—were the scholars of Wissenschaft des Judentums. Conversely, those who perpetuated the neglect of history were Dubnow's fellow eastern European Jews, whom he excoriated for failing to collect, organize, and analyze the rich sources their ancestors had left behind. The stakes were high, as Dubnow acknowledged: "We have sinned against history. The time has come to release it and to reconstruct the remains of its ruins."[50]

Over the next half-century, until his tragic death in 1941, Dubnow would shift the focus of his critique. As he refined his own historical method, he increasingly sought to escape the emphases of German-Jewish scholarship, and especially those of the influential macrohistorian who preceded him, Heinrich Graetz. In introducing his own multivolume history in 1925,

Dubnow heralded the advent of a secular nationalist movement which would have a profound effect on historiography, "liberating it from the shackles of theology and, subsequently, of spiritualism or scholasticism."[51]

This impulse to unhinge Jewish scholarship from its dependence on Wissenschaft des Judentums extended well beyond Dubnow and his form of nationalism. His friend and polemical partner, the prominent Zionist and Hebrew essayist Ahad Ha-am, who was not a professional scholar but rather a highly informed consumer of scholarship, set the stage for the Zionist drive for historiographical liberation. He declared in the journal *Ha-Shiloah* in 1902 that "the most diligent and original workers in this field [Jewish studies] are Gentile scholars, from whose wells Jewish scholars drink and in whose footsteps they walk." He went on to lament, in terms that evoke the traditionalist Zeev Jawitz, that Wissenschaft des Judentums is "beholden to the reign of aliens," which prevents "the original Jewish spirit from being revealed in all its originality, as we are entitled to hope for."[52]

Ahad Ha-am's successor as editor of the Odessa-based *Ha-Shiloah*, Yosef Klausner, who *was* a Heidelberg-trained professional scholar, sought to overcome this deficiency. He announced a call in *Ha-Shiloah*'s pages to create a *mada 'ivri*, a scientific scholarship in Hebrew that would be free of both foreign influence and dilettantish poseurs, while attaining a high standard of research excellence.[53] In 1919, Klausner emigrated from Odessa to Palestine, where he became a founding member of the faculty of the Hebrew University of Jerusalem when it opened in 1925.

Klausner and his new colleagues were confident that the move to Jerusalem from Europe, from which almost all of them came, would free scholarship from slavish dependence and bias. They were hardly a uniform lot. They came from different parts of the Continent. They included piously observant and proudly secular figures. They disagreed passionately with one another about politics. And they represented a wide range of disciplinary interests. But they shared the conviction that Jerusalem had the potential to alter the way in which the past was understood. The most renowned member of this founding generation of "Jerusalem scholars," Gershom Scholem, insisted that the "return" of Jewish scholars to Jerusalem afforded an altogether novel "historic perspective from within." For his own field of research, Jewish mysticism, this new perspective provided an opportunity "to create something out of nothing . . . to estimate the true value of the religious movement known as Kabbala, and to assess the correct position to be assigned to it in the life and history of our people."[54] Meanwhile, the historians Yitzhak Baer and Ben Zion Dinur maintained that the move to Jerusalem would liberate Jewish scholarship from the "theological-literary" orientation of Wissenschaft des Judentums. This meant a dramatic restaging of Jewish history; its main protagonist was no longer Judaism the religion. Rather, as Baer and Dinur declared in the pages of the nascent journal *Zion,* "Jewish history is the history of the Jewish [Israelite] nation."[55]

The Jerusalem historians, separated by background and temperament, joined in the goal of identifying previously submerged nationalist currents in the Jewish past. As I noted in the introduction, Baer traced in *Galut* a lineage of thinkers throughout Jewish history who recognized the ignominy of exile and the concomitant virtue of return to the homeland. Meanwhile, in his last book, *Yisra'el ba-'amim* (Israel Among the Nations), he uncovered a pious democratic spirit that, he believed, inspired and preserved a national sense among the Jews from the time of the Second Temple. He concluded by asserting an unbroken chain of collective identity: "In the end, several grand pillars of the mystical-historical edifice of the ancients will remain—pillars which the first *Hasidim* planted in the soil of Erets Yisra'el, which are rooted in the heart of every man, and through which the future place of Israel among the nations will be recorded."[56]

Baer can hardly be reduced to a crass ideologue masquerading as a historian. He was an eminent Hispanist with an encyclopedic grasp of the Spanish archives, as well as expertise in many other areas of history. At the same time, he was intent on using history to deepen a sense of connection to the past—indeed, to excavate pillars of memory for future generations. He highlighted the painful memory of *galut*, the antidote to which was the liberating act of return to the Land of Israel. This impulse was hardly his alone. It was shared by Baer's colleague in Jerusalem, Dinur, who was the most unabashedly ideological of his cohort there. In his wide-ranging collections of sources, Dinur charted the persistent allure of the Land of Israel for Jews in the Diaspora, including in his multivolume *Yisra'el ba-Golah* (Israel in the Diaspora). This "Palestinocentric" tendency, in which the Land of Israel was the central axis around which Jewish history revolved, prompted Dinur to forage through the past to identify Zionists *avant la lettre*, Jews who left their home countries for Palestine prior to the advent of Zionism. At the same time, he also sought to chronicle the norms, habits, and practices—what he called the "socio-psychological" dimension—of Jews that preserved "common memories of the nation" in the Diaspora.[57]

Collecting the documentary traces of these memories and using them to foster a deeper connection to the past defined Dinur's calling, both as a historian and as a public official. Never content to remain in the narrow corridors of the academy, he assumed a variety of official roles, including Israeli minister of education (1951–1955). In that role he was able to shape popular historical education through curriculum development, textbooks, and teacher training, in particular focusing on Palestine as the guiding axis of Jewish history. Moreover, he fostered in his work, in the tradition of historians committed to nationalist causes, a sense of the distinctive historical path of his people.[58] In emphasizing this point, Dinur was not interested merely in proving the ongoing link of Jews to the Land of Israel; he also felt it imperative to contrast this to the position of Palestinian Arabs, who "have all rights [in the State of Israel], but over the Land of Israel have no right." This distinction between the civil rights of Arabs and the historical right of Jews to the land was frequently uttered by political leaders, especially David Ben-Gurion, who affirmed as early as 1929 that "Arabs have full rights as citizens of the country, but they do not have the right of ownership over it."[59] On this view, the right of ownership belonged to the Jews, whose ancient roots in Palestine granted them primogeniture in the present. Of course, it is not only the Jews who make historical claims replete with current political consequences. Palestinians do as well, asserting their own claim to the Haram al-Sharif (Temple Mount) in Jerusalem—and their rights to Palestine—while denying implicitly or explicitly a Jewish connection.[60]

While noting the consequential and somewhat uncomfortable alliance of history and politics in and around Jerusalem, it is also worth noting that the founding "Jerusalem scholars" laid a solid institutional foundation for what has become over the course of ninety years the largest and most influential center of Jewish historical scholarship in the world. Moreover, they opened many new lines of intellectual inquiry, exploring new subject areas, sources, methods, and emphases—Kabbalah and Jewish mysticism, Hebrew language and literature, archaeology and biblical studies, and the history and topography of Palestine, among others. They were inspired by the belief that the work of tapping into the wellsprings of Jewish history could feed the living currents of Jewish life in the present.

A similar sense of the vitalizing potential of scholarship was shared by the ideological rivals of the Zionists, the adepts of

Yiddish who created YIVO, the main center of scholarship in Yiddish, in 1925. They held important organizing meetings in Vilna in the same period as the formal opening of the Hebrew University on 1 April 1925.[61] A related and, to an extent, competing circle was also discussing the future of Yiddish-based scholarship in Berlin, where many eastern European Jews had come after the First World War. The various Yiddish activist-scholars represented a parallel universe of sorts to the scholarly and institutional activity in Jerusalem, though one in which some of the Jerusalem scholars such as Dinur had earlier dwelt but from which they had since exited. For several decades, they and their forebears had been engaged in a range of disciplinary pursuits—history, philology and literature, ethnography—under the rubric *yidishe visnshaft* ("Jewish scholarship" in Yiddish).[62]

Notwithstanding their ideological differences with the Jerusalem scholars, the Yiddish scholarly activists started from a familiar point of action; they too aspired to liberate themselves from their predecessors. Nokhem Shtif, a Ukrainian-born literary and historical scholar and the driving force behind the Berlin-based efforts, gave clear voice to this sentiment. In his lapidary manifesto of 1925, "On a Yiddish Scientific Institute," he opened with a call reminiscent of many previous Jewish scholars: the time had come for the Jews to take part in the larger scholarly world by creating their own first-rate institutions. And yet, in a curious twist, he subverted the oft-invoked hierarchy between German and eastern European Jews—*Yekkes* and *Ostjuden*. He declared that the new Yiddish scholarship marked "an emancipation from the ghetto circle of scholarly interests that the activists of 'Wissenschaft des Judentums' cultivate."[63] Not only were the earlier German scholars uninterested in Yiddish itself; they were, as Shtif claimed, "fundamentally hostile to the cultural interest of the Jewish masses, their language, (and) their living social and cultural creativity."[64] What was required was a reinvigoration of Jewish scholarship, to be executed, as with the Jerusalem scholars, by a new scholarly focus not on the dead past but on the living, vibrant Jewish people. The next two decades witnessed a rich outpouring of scholarship in Yiddish, some based at YIVO in Vilna and some elsewhere. Figures such as Jacob Lestshinsky, Raphael Mahler, Emanuel Ringelblum, Ignacy Schiper, and Elias Tcherikower charted new ground both by refining a modern scholarly idiom in Yiddish and by investigating the largely unexplored social, material, and demographic history of eastern European Jewry. Like their colleagues, friends, and rivals in Jerusalem, the Yiddish scholars mobilized scholarship to craft a new image and memory of the Jewish past as a prelude to a promising future. As a rule, the two groups were far less inhibited than their Wissenschaft forebears in Germany in moving back and forth between careful monographic labor and educational, cultural, and political activities in the public domain.

LIBERATION FROM PATRIARCHAL DOMINATION

We have seen how scholars of Jewish history often availed themselves of the potential to disrupt, affirm, or recraft received narratives in order to set in place a serviceable image or memory of the past. In parallel, they sought to liberate the past on behalf of a diverse range of causes: theological supersession, political emancipation, religious reform, traditionalist revival, and national awakening. While there are many engaged scholars who are not historians, and many historians who are not inclined to be engaged, the discipline of history does seem to have a special purchase on public engagement, given its ability to liberate from the prejudices of the past. Our focus to this point has been on male historians writing in the nineteenth and early twentieth centuries. We now turn to two contemporary female scholars for whom history served as an instrument of liberation from past patterns of male domination and oppression. In general, scholars of women's and gender history have been especially attuned to the potential of their discipline to identify deficiencies from the past and propose alternatives for the future.[65]

The first of the two is Gerda Lerner, who blazed a pioneering trail in her wide-ranging research, as well as in introducing women's history into the curricula of university history departments across the United States. Lerner understood as well as any "why history matters," as she framed an especially thoughtful essay from a 1997 collection of that name. One of the most intriguing features of that essay was her comparison of two groups—indeed, "the two groups," she noted, "which have for the longest time in human history been marginalized and oppressed—women and Jews." Significantly, this comparison yielded not merely similarities (for example, their common experience of oppression) but also key differences, one of which was that for Jews, historical memory was "a prime tool of survival." Women, by contrast, were deprived of the capacity to "share in creating the mental constructs that explain and order the world, a world in which they lived but whose annals they were prevented from recording.[66] But the historian could now play that role.

Herein lay the liberatory potential of women's history, of which women were both its objects and, to a great extent, its ideal subjects. As Lerner explained, "When women discover their history and learn their connectedness to the past and to the human social enterprise, their consciousness is inevitably and dramatically transformed. This experience is for them transcendent, in that it enables them to perceive what they share and always have shared with other women." Women's history, she continued, was "the essential tool in creating feminist consciousness in women." And that consciousness was a vital link to women's empowerment. In this way, Lerner argued, "The past becomes part of our present and thereby part of our future." And the historian plays a crucial role as a bridge between the times. Indeed, it is the historian who has the ability to connect the recovery of a forgotten past to the realization of women's agency in the future.[67]

Lerner devoted most of her important scholarly labors to women's history. But the connection between her professional path and family origins was unmistakable: "I am a historian," she wrote, "because of my Jewish experience."[68] It was that experience, punctuated by her own theological doubts and the deep scar of Nazism, that inculcated in her an awareness of the benefits and deficits of difference. And it led her to return periodically to a comparison of women and Jews, with both of whom she identified to varying extents and both of whose historical paths she traced in their diverging and occasionally converging routes.

The theme of comparing women's and Jewish history brings us to our final example of historian qua liberator, the late Yale scholar Paula Hyman. Hyman was deeply committed to the study of both fields or, more particularly, to the intersection of the two. Although she roamed widely in her research, from her early studies on Jews in France to later work on the United States, Poland, and Palestine, Hyman had an increasingly strong interest over the latter half of her career in pushing to the surface the oft-marginalized experience of Jewish women. A good indication of this interest was her iconic article from 1982 on the kosher meat boycott organized by immigrant Jewish women in New York in 1902. She began the article on the boycott by declaring that "women have always participated in politics."[69] Left unsaid, but clearly intended, was the fact that their participation has not always been counted in the historical record, a deficiency she set out to repair.

Less than a decade later, when she had the opportunity to summarize her thoughts in a 1991 volume edited by Judith Baskin, *Jewish Women in Historical Perspective,* Hyman observed that "in much of American Jewish historiography women make scarcely more than a cameo appearance."[70] Her mission thus became, as she put it in her synthesizing *Gender and Assimilation in Modern Jewish History* (1995), to explore and reclaim a role for women in the Jewish past, while challenging old, male-dominated historiographical conventions.[71] For Hyman, as both Jewish historian and Jewish feminist, the impulse to set in place a historical memory of women and women's agency in the narrative of Jewish history was an act of methodological and political liberation, consistent with her desire to overcome the prejudices of the past as a means of assuring a more equitable future for women.

Hyman came of age in the sixties and seventies, a time of great cultural, social, and gender upheaval in American life. Antiwar activity, social protest, Jewish renewal, and feminism were all part of her world, in which scholarly integrity and identify formation were complementary, not oppositional. In her own life, Hyman looked for inspiration to Puah Rakovsky, the radical Russian-Jewish memoirist whom she studied: that is, as "a role model, demonstrating that women could have an impact on the Jewish and general communities."[72] In noting this, we should recall that Hyman was not a unidimensional activist beholden only to one realm of activity. Nor were most of the historians we have explored in this chapter. Their commitments were multifarious and overlapping, converging in their vision of bringing scholarship to life. As a whole, these historians-cum-liberators challenge the claim that virtuous history demands scrupulous avoidance of the present or the complete extinguishing of the self. Rather, they affirm that history is a demanding practice with its own exacting protocol, but it can also be a powerful agent of change as well as of preservation. Indeed, historians call on the past to affirm or re-create webs of memory in which they themselves are enmeshed. In the next chapter, we will focus on the desire not to break free from a stubborn past but to tap into it as a source of consolation in the present.

2

History as Consolation

Two years after the publication of *Zakhor*, Yosef Yerushalmi delivered a lecture at the Colloque des intellectuels juifs de langue française in Paris titled "Vers une histoire de l'espoir juif." In this 1984 talk, he drew up a blueprint for a future project in the mode of the French *Annales* school that would explore the long "history of Jewish hope." He was interested in examining the various modes by which Jews contended with the challenges, disappointments, and persecution that accompanied their long historical journey. While outbreaks of active messianism were fueled by the hope of immediate liberation, it was not that explosive form of hope that interested him. Rather, he called attention to the more routine, even daily practices, what he called the "interim Jewish hopes for the times before the end of Time." These embodied a certain elasticity that permitted Jews to see themselves as part of an inextinguishable heritage. Hope, in this sense, grew out of despair, a despair born of frequent travails. Indeed, the longue durée of Jewish suffering yielded a history of hope. Yerushalmi concluded his lecture by offering his own rationale for undertaking a history of hope: "To assuage our loneliness. To realize that we are not the first to whom despair was not alien, nor hope a gratuitous gift, and that by the same token we are not necessarily the last. And that, perhaps, may be a small and modest step toward hope itself."[1] Yerushalmi made passing reference to historical writing as a vehicle of hope, though he did not fully assess its role. He did consider, however, the idea that Jews had developed a technique over time, a "midrash of history," that allowed past traumas to be interpreted in such a way as to "endure and overcome them." The midrash of history could offer a measure of consolation based on the faith and staying power of the Jews.[2]

In general, when people have sought consolation for their predicament or fate, they have relied on forms of writing other than history, such as liturgy, poetry, belles lettres and even philosophy, which the sixth-century Roman Boethius used to assuage his despair as he awaited imminent capital punishment.[3] In fact, in investigating the place of history as a source of consolation, I found only a *single* entry in the catalogue of the Library of Congress. An early-twentieth-century literary scholar by the name of Frederick Tupper delivered an after-dinner toast at the annual banquet of the Vermont Commandery of the Loyal Legion of the United States on 11 May 1920 that was published as "The Consolation of History." Drawing on the relatively recent experience of the Civil War and the immediately concluded Great War, Tupper noted the mix of destruction, woe, and dysfunction that followed serious military conflict. Why recount this misery? Tupper responded to his own question: "We should find small comfort in the thought that other men and other times had suffered like ourselves, save for the ensuing reflection that, in each period, the darkness is followed by a golden dawn and a blue day."[4]

It is this very sentiment that surfaces frequently in Jewish historical writing, forming a unit of the history of hope that Yerushalmi imagined. In this chapter I shall examine how Jewish chroniclers and historians have used the historical medium to console, extending from the biblical era and late antiquity through the Middle Ages to the modern era. This longer-term angle will grant us greater perspective on the function of the Jewish historical writer in the transition from amateur chronicler to professional historian. It will also lend perspective on my opening claim that history, even in its modern guise, should not be seen in opposition to memory. Indeed, both modern and premodern recorders have committed to recalling episodes of past despair and hope as a means of institutionalizing memory. In this way, historically informed memory became a prime repository of consolation in its various guises, which range from the life-affirming to the lachrymose, from the self-effacing to the mocking, from the cyclical to the linear, and from the therapeutic to the obsessive.

COLLECTING TRAGEDY

In a series of books published in the 1980s, two important American scholars of Jewish literature, David Roskies and Alan Mintz, collected and studied the abundant texts produced in the wake of tragedies that have befallen the Jews. Roskies observed that these texts permitted Jews to "perceive the cyclical nature of violence and find some measure of comfort in the repeatability of the unprecedented." Whereas traditional religious sources performed these functions throughout much of Jewish history, in the modern age, Roskies adverts, "history itself became a moral reference point for secular Jews who no longer attended synagogue or accepted the claims of Jewish sacred chronology."[5]

Roskies follows the work of previous scholars, particularly Nathan Wachtel and Paul Fussell, in suggesting that "the response of individuals and collectives to crisis situations is governed by preexisting patterns." Of particular relevance is Fussell, whose 1975 *The Great War and Modern Memory* was a signal achievement in efforts to understand the vast impact of the First World War, including its reshaping of the very category and parameters of memory. The recurrence of certain flora and fauna in writing of the era prompted Fussell to observe that "one notices and remembers what one has been 'coded'—usually by literature or its popular equivalent—to notice and remember."[6]

In the forty years since Fussell offered his insight about the coded nature of our memories, there has been a veritable revolution in our understanding of how memory follows preexisting patterns.[7] Neuroscientists have been working to piece together the ways neurons contain and store memory. The physical process of recollecting, they believe, actually carves out neural pathways that "become stronger the more they are used, causing the likelihood of new long-term connections and memories."[8] The more we recall a certain event or personality, the more well-trodden become the pathways.

Neuroscience helps us understand this process of memory formation in the individual brain. But it cannot unpack the mysteries of collective memory, since groups do not possess a single set of neurons, cortices, and synapses. How then to speak of collective memory? Maurice Halbwachs observed that "while the collective memory endures and draws strength from its base in a coherent body of people, it is individuals as group members who remember."[9] But they do so as part of a social network such that "collective memory is more than just an aggregate of individuals' personal memories."[10]

Although not possessed of a single brain, groups do forge memories based on the performance of shared rituals of commemoration, exposure to common education, and family storytelling. And metaphorically, we might say that the recurrence of these recollections carves out pathways of what we might call collective memory.[11] To be sure, this ever-swirling mix of memory acts is not fixed in stone; it is subject to what Ernest Renan called a "daily plebiscite," a shifting constellation of opinion, sentiment, and disposition.

And yet, while shifting, this constellation is not altogether evanescent. It represents the shared memory of the nation at a given point of time. In the case of a group such as the Jews, the pathways of their socially constructed memory have been repeatedly paved by ritualized recollection that has fallen into certain archetypal patterns: covenantal relationship with God, tragedy, redemption.

To capture the depth of the tracks of Jewish memory, we extend back to antiquity to notice the role that biblical prophets played as both admonishers and consolers. As an archetype, the prophet Jeremiah, witness to the destruction of the First Temple, excelled in warning of the consequences of recalcitrance and misdeeds. By disobeying the Lord, he admonished the Judeans, "you shall die by the sword, by the famine, and by pestilence in the place where you want to go and sojourn" (Jer. 42:22). By contrast, Isaiah, or rather the array of authors presumed to have written under that name, offered assurance that the Jews, by virtue of their chosenness, would not be abandoned in times of need. God's message, as conveyed through Isaiah, was unmistakable: "They who strive with you shall become as naught and shall perish." To leave little doubt, Isaiah records these consoling words: "For I the LORD am your God, Who grasped your right hand, Who say to you: Have no fear; I will be your help" (Isa. 41:11, 13).[12]

Consolation was inextricably linked to recollection of past travails in biblical sources. The relentless tide of misfortune that befell the once wealthy Job could not destroy his sense of appreciation at surviving. As Paul Ricouer observed in his powerfully Christian reading of the concept, consolation resulted from Job's recognition that our existence is a function of God's majestic power to which all must submit.[13] That quality of submission figured in some, but not all, subsequent forms of Jewish consolation. Anger, revenge, and pride were also common motifs in the consolatory literature of the Jews, which surfaced in the wake of the frequent crises they faced.

One such case is Josephus, the first-century general and historian mentioned in the previous chapter as the source of inspiration for Jacques Basnage and Hannah Adams. Josephus, who switched loyalties from the Jewish to the Roman side during the Great Revolt, wrote a seminal historical account of it, *The Jewish War,* that included a fair measure of self-consolation. Through his unsparing condemnation of the fanaticism of some Jewish contemporaries, he could rationalize his own decision to shift loyalties in the late stages of the conflict in the year 70.

But more germane to our concerns might be a later book that Josephus wrote (perhaps by borrowing heavily from another author), *Against Apion,* aimed at the anti-Jewish agitator of that name who sought to persuade the emperor Caligula of Jewish perfidy and disloyalty in the year 40. More than a half-century after the event, Josephus penned a response, a work of polemics and apologetics, and a clear instance of history as consolation— and by extension, hope. Josephus began by challenging a rather commonplace assumption in his day that it was the Greeks, not the Jews, who were possessed of a long and noble history. Josephus states simply that "their nation was *not* ancient," referring to the Greeks, who, he reminded readers, were conspicuously absent from any biblical sources. By contrast, he avails himself of Egyptian, Phoenician, and, compellingly, Greek accounts to demonstrate the antiquity of the Jews. He does so not only to disabuse Greeks of their mistaken sense of superiority but also to remind Jews of the antiquity and dignity of their own past in the wake of calumnious accusations against them.[14]

Notwithstanding the ongoing inner conflict between his Jewish and Roman selves, Josephus seeks here to console. Like earlier and later Jewish historical consolers, he is moved to take up the writing of history after a major crisis—in this case, the destruction of the Second Temple. That said, his sober tone is very different in tenor from the previous prophetic model, which relied on the active presence of God, or from the exhortatory examples that begin to appear a millennium later.

One of the most notable cases in this regard is the spate of Hebrew chronicles written in the wake of the Crusader violence directed against Ashkenazic Jewish communities that began in 1096. It should be noted that there has been a long and intense debate over the veracity of the chronicles, particularly over whether they are an accurate reflection of the sentiments of the day or a projection of later sensibilities onto the events themselves.[15] The task here is not to engage this theoretical and historical question but rather to grasp the consolatory character of the medieval Hebrew chronicles, whose expressive mode of writing differs markedly from Josephus's *Against Apion*. There is no pretense here of a careful sifting of evidence, such as the ancient historian offered. Rather, the medieval Hebrew chronicles convey an unmistakable sense of the election of the Jews, as well as the unique travails to which they were subjected. They also articulate in ways familiar to the midrashic imagination of late antiquity an uncommon range of emotions, including bewilderment and even anger at God: "God, the maker of peace, turned aside and averted His eyes from His people, and consigned them to the sword," declared the twelfth-century chronicle of Solomon bar Shimson. The chronicler continued with evident consternation: "No prophet, seer, or man of wise heart was able to comprehend how the sin of the people infinite in number was deemed so great as to cause the destruction of so many lives in the various Jewish communities."[16]

Not content to leave the final verdict to God, the chronicler audaciously compared the mass murder of Jews by Crusaders to the binding of Isaac, except that in the later case there were "one thousand one hundred offerings in one single day." Of course, in bloody contrast to the biblical Isaac, the father's knife *did* fall on the neck of a large number of Rhineland Jews. As martyrs or, as the Hebrew term *kidush ha-Shem* connotes, as sanctifiers of the name of God, though, they did not die in vain. The chronicler summons forth the hope and expectation, echoed in the companion account of Rabbi Eliezer bar Nathan, that "their merit, their righteousness, their piety, their whole-heartedness, and their sacrifice be a good advocate for us before the Most High" so as to "deliver us from the exile of wicked Edom speedily in our Day."[17]

At one level, this salvific postmortem follows a well-carved pathway of Jewish memory: tragedy is followed by introspection, internalization of guilt, and then renewed faith in divine munificence. In adhering to the general contours of this script, the chronicler's account of martyrdom, Ivan Marcus observes, "is legitimated by being masked in archetypal symbolism" culled from the Bible.[18] And yet, the Hebrew Crusade chroniclers invest their protagonists with a degree of courage and virtue surpassing that even of revered ancient heroes such as Isaac or Rabbi Akiba. The usual self-chastisement is conveyed with a measure of disbelief, and indeed is subordinate to the bold claim that those killed were worthy martyrs. For the chroniclers, martyrdom of this sort mandates vengeance, which is a prelude to and companion of redemption. In proposing this causal chain of martyrdom-vengeance-redemption, the chronicle is intended to reassure, model ideal behavior for, and *console* the survivors of the Crusader violence.[19]

We do not have, it must be said, a clear sense of the nature or scale of the audience of these chronicles, especially in the twelfth and thirteenth centuries. It is highly improbable that manuscript copies of the chronicles made their way to the homes of many Jews of the era. And yet, over time, the chronicles did become—along with other rituals, liturgical forms, fast and feast days, and memorial books—an important pillar of the historical memory of Ashkenazic Jewry.[20] This memory was laced with examples of death and destruction, such that martyrdom became a recurrent and even cherished ideal for gen-

erations of Ashkenazim. Indeed, subsequent tragedies that befell them—the mass murders in Chmielnicki of 1648–1649, the
massacre of Humań (Uman) of 1768, the Ukrainian pogroms of
1918–1919—were seen as part of a continuous historical tradition.[21]

Curiously then, the knowledge that other members of the group
have suffered before, coupled with the realization that Jews as a
collective have survived, has served as consolation to survivors
and their descendants. Indeed, this mix of the mournful and the
triumphalist is characteristic of Ashkenazic historical memory,
but it is not unique to it.[22]

Several hundred years later, in a different milieu and respon-
sive to a different set of historical circumstances, the enigmatic
Sephardic savant Samuel Usque wrote a work in Portuguese titled *Consolation for the Tribulations of Israel* (1553).[23] We know
very little about the sixteenth-century author, but it is clear
that he intended his *Consolation* for those, like himself, who
were forcibly converted, or whose forbears had been forcibly
converted, to Christianity in the Iberian Peninsula. Like many
of his fellow conversos, Usque was worldly and at home in lan-
guages and literatures of the world. But in contrast to most, he
had an uncommonly good grasp of Hebrew and postbiblical
Jewish literature, as well as a masterful command of the Bible.
He used this unique blend of knowledge to construct a sweeping history of Jewish travails, from ancient times to his own
day, cast in a pastoral trialogue typical of the Renaissance era.
His main protagonists were three shepherds, Ycabo, Zicareo,
and Numeo, whose names harked back to biblical heroes. As
Martin Cohen has examined in his meticulous edition of the
Consolation, Ycabo, or Jacob, narrates the long and sad series of
disasters to befall the Jews.[24] Zicareo, whose name recalls the
prophet Zechariah and gestures to the Hebrew verb "to remember" (*z-kh-r*), summons up past examples of God's ongoing devotion to the Jewish people. And Numeo, whose Hebrew name

comes from the root for "consolation" and evokes the scribe Nehemiah, delivers precisely that in response to Ycabo. The final section of the book, which details the medieval and early modern tribulations of the Jews from Persia to Germany, concludes with a long soliloquy by Numeo that enumerates eight sources of consolation. Among them was the patronage of Doña Gracia Nasi (Mendes), the wealthy Portuguese-born conversa who immigrated to Italy via Antwerp and then, with the Inquisition on her heels, to Constantinople. Wherever she settled, she provided her generous material support to Jews, especially former conversos seeking to return to an open Jewish life. Usque, who referred to Doña Gracia as "the very illustrious lady," dedicated his book to her.[25]

Just as with the Crusade chronicles, we do not know how widely read or distributed the *Consolation for the Tribulations of Israel* was. One might speculate that the text was passed around in samizdat fashion in communities where former Portuguese-speaking conversos were to be found throughout Europe, the Mediterranean region, and later the Americas. What we do know is that Usque employed the multitudinous woes of the past to point up the survival of the Jews and thereby affirm the election of Israel. As a reflection of his hope for the future, he took the next logical step by framing the persecution-laden history of the Jews as an extended prelude to the imminent coming of the Messiah. Indeed, the redemptive passion of his shepherd-narrators courses powerfully through the entire book.

Unlike other contemporaneous books of historical content such as Solomon ibn Verga's *Shevet Yehudah* or Azariah de' Rossi's *Me'or 'eynayim*, Usque's *Consolation* did not presage an incipient modern historicism in terms of mundane causality. Its pastoral frame and unabashedly didactic quality are strikingly different from the form and content of modern historiography.[26] Or so it would seem based on the assumption of a deep chasm between the rich fabric of premodern collective memory and the sober quality of modern critical history.

TEARS OF CONSOLATION IN THE MODERN AGE

In his iconic article of 1928, "Ghetto and Emancipation," Salo W. Baron introduced the memorable notion of a long-regnant "lachrymose theory" informing Jewish history, according to which modern scholars were drawn to the tragedies of the Jews like flies to light. The historian David Engel has recently reminded us that Baron directed his critique of the lachrymose theory at overly dark renderings of *the period prior to the modern age*. Baron in fact believed that Jews had a relatively good life in medieval times, certainly better than the average peasant or serf, since they were afforded protection by sovereigns who valued their presence as economic assets and permitted them to dwell safely within their own religious communities.[27]

By contrast, modernity exposed Jews, Baron continued, to many more challenges and obstacles than cheery champions of the Enlightenment were willing to admit. He was attentive to the manifold threats—the surprising persistence of physical violence and the unraveling of communal ties at the hands of liberal individualism—that undermined Jewish life in the modern age. Baron's reversal of the commonplace historical assumption of the darkness of the Middle Ages and the lightness of the Enlightenment helps us understand why consolation and its partner, lachrymosity, persisted as themes in modern Jewish history and historical thought. While we might have expected them to disappear, at least until the Holocaust, both surfaced frequently in modern times. Accordingly, the boundary between early modern chroniclers and modern historians becomes more porous than we might otherwise imagine.

This is not to suggest a complete identity between them,

for there are fundamental differences in the use of sources and causal logic. But when meditating on the task of history, or of the historian, we cannot avoid the conclusion that the wheel was not invented in modernity. This recalls the view articulated by Karl Löwith in his 1949 *Meaning in History*. There he asserted that modern philosophies of history, from the Enlightenment to Marxism, draw upon and seek to secularize traditional Christian *Heilsgeschichte* (sacred history).[28] It may be possible to take an additional step beyond Löwith and his identification of a shared teleological structure to past and present historical perspectives. Behind its dispassionate modern facade, history has an emotional register and affective presence that moves, urges to action, and consoles, much as did medieval and early modern historical writing (though at times with a different sense of causal agency).

One of the key issues that purveyors of Jewish history, modern and premodern, had to contend with was the seemingly cyclical nature of the past: historical organisms that rose up before falling into decline. Cyclical approaches to the past often portended a pessimistic view of history; a long line of thinkers, from the ancient Greeks to moderns such as Oswald Spengler and Arnold Toynbee, concluded that the arc of history—and in some specific cases, of Jewish history—moved toward decline.

There were scholars of the Jewish past, principally, Christian supersessionists such as Basnage and Hannah Adams, who believed that the arc of Jewish history did indeed head downward after the destruction of the Second Temple. A competing group of modern Jewish scholars, while mindful of the momentous nature of the events of 70 C.E., argued otherwise by juxtaposing the disappearance of other groups from the stage of history to the unlikely durability of the Jews. In this sense, they embraced a consolatory role for history, as had their precursors.

Among them was the intriguing nineteenth-century Jewish

thinker, less a historian than a philosopher of history, Nachman Krochmal. Krochmal was a Galician-born scholar whose Hebrew magnum opus was *A Guide for the Perplexed of the Time* (*More nevukhe ha-zeman*). He suffered the fate of many of his fellow yeshiva students who were all too aware of the finitude of their Talmudic erudition; that is, he excelled in the oral arts but left little in written or published form. Fortunately, he entrusted to his colleague and friend Leopold Zunz the task of producing a posthumous edition of the sprawling *Guide*.

Over the course of his lifetime, Krochmal read widely and deeply in European philosophy, though he never attended university. Especially notable in his *Guide* was the prevalence of two core concepts embedded in modern European thought: the idea of a guiding "spirit" of history and the notion of cycles in history. The two ideas were central to the work of prominent European philosophers—Giambattista Vico, J. G. Herder, G. W. F. Hegel—who were among the key sources in framing his thinking.[29] In particular, the cyclical scheme of history was important to his larger mission in the *Guide*. It was a weapon in the debate among Enlightenment and post-Enlightenment thinkers in the late eighteenth and early nineteenth centuries over whether Judaism was dead or alive, "fossil or phoenix," to borrow Shlomo Avineri's phrase.[30]

In contrast to his philosophical foil, Hegel, for instance, Krochmal did not hold to a declensionist view of Jewish history. Rather, he employed the concept of a guiding spirit, akin to Hegel's Absolute Spirit, to combat the view that Jews would rise or fall—or indeed, had already risen or fallen—like other nations. The nations of the world, he explained in the eighth chapter of his *Guide*, passed through the same three phases of growth, maturation, and decline. But "regarding our nation," he continued, "both in relation to the material dimension and to the externality of the senses, we have submitted to the natural order mentioned above [the cycles of history]. At the same time, it is as the Sages of blessed memory said: 'When they were exiled in Babylon, the Shekhinah went with them (b. Meg. 29a); when they were exiled in Elam, the Shekhinah went with them.' Thus, the general Spirit within us will protect us and *save us from the fate of other passing nations*" (emphasis added). Whereas other nations rose and fell, the Jews were different: "If we fall, we arise anew and are fortified, for the Lord our God never leaves us."[31] In his abstruse philosophical style, Krochmal provided a measure of hope by lifting the Jewish people above the gravitational pull of time-bound history into a realm of transcendence guarded over by the God of Israel.

Why, we might reasonably ask. If the Crusade chroniclers sought to provide solace to the heirs of the martyrs of 1096, and Usque to liberated conversos, what did Krochmal seek to offer? He was speaking to a different generation of Jews in the early nineteenth century, caught between the allure of an open and enlightened world and the stark reality of ongoing obstacles on the path toward it. In this new and charged universe, the Jews had become the subject of intense debate revolving around nothing less than the merits of their continuation. Krochmal proposed his own answer to the question of Jewish survival, availing himself of a new philosophical idiom to convey an old message: namely, that Jews soared above the plane of mundane history on which the rest of the nations rose and fell.

It would seem easy to dismiss this kind of metahistorical exceptionalism as the product of a traditionalist rabbi seeking to provide an anchor of stability in the churning waters of his day—indeed, as an adumbration of the contemporary Orthodox popularizer Rabbi Berel Wein. One could also point out that Jews of Krochmal's own day did not derive any benefit from his attempt at historical consolation, since his *Guide for the Perplexed of the Time* was published eleven years after he died.

But these claims do not do justice to Krochmal's wide-ranging knowledge, sophistication, and prominence, at least among the scholarly elite of central and east central European Jewry. Nor, more importantly for our purposes, do they take stock of the recurrent appeals to the transcendence of Jewish history—not by traditionalist rabbis, of whom Krochmal was not really an example, but by their presumed opposites, avowed secularists, who adopted the consoling function of earlier chroniclers.

The received wisdom, anchored by Yerushalmi's claims in *Zakhor*, is that the first modern Jewish historians, as a result of their new university training, cultural sensibilities, and oft-thwarted desire for integration, were increasingly detached from the currents of collective memory. Their declared loyalty was to Wissenschaft, to objectivity, and to acceptance by the broader community of scholars. Neither providing consolation nor instilling hope was the aim, as it had been for earlier chroniclers.

The story is more complicated, as Yerushalmi's own earlier and later work demonstrates. So too, Ismar Schorsch and Michael Meyer, among the most prominent of German-Jewish historians, identify threads of continuity between previous renderings of Jewish history and those of the Wissenschaft des Judentums circle. Schorsch, for his part, insists that Jewish memory and historical consciousness were altered but not destroyed by the age of emancipation. Meyer uncovers "persistent tensions" between scholarly and existential or communal concerns in early Wissenschaft des Judentums.[32] From the time of Leopold Zunz, German-Jewish scholars used the medium of history to promote, defend, and polemicize on behalf of (or, less frequently, against) their community. First-generation Wissenschaft scholars advocated in support of the emancipation of the Jews. The next generation turned the scholarly medium inward to advance an array of religious denominational agendas. The following generation utilized an array of historical tools to assert the antiquity of Jewish residence on German soil as a means of combating antisemitism.[33] The relevance of history in this milieu was not simply to serve as a bulwark against the erosion of memory in the modern age, against what Pierre Nora called the "increasingly rapid slippage of the present into a historical past that is gone for good."[34] It was also to provide a shield of protection to Jews in an age of forceful anti-Jewish sentiment.[35]

But history served not just as a cudgel of defense. It also was explicitly summoned up to fortify memory and provide consolation—and in ways that reveal the use and potential abuse of history. One of the sites of history's consoling function in this period was the revived legacy of Crusader violence against medieval Jewry. As a general matter, leading Jewish scholars such as Zunz, Graetz, and Simon Dubnow, writing at different times and places, focused attention in their historical writings on the devastating effects of the Crusades on Ashkenazic Jewry.[36] In the wake of the eight hundredth anniversary of the outbreak of the Crusades in 1896, the German rabbi and researcher Siegmund Salfeld edited a collection of sources relating to persecutions in German lands from 1096 to 1348, expressing the hope that it might serve as "a monument to a period of Jewish suffering, erected in piety and love."[37] Zeev Jawitz, for his part, waxed poetic in his *Toldot Yisra'el* about the "grandeur and heroism that shone through the darkness and destruction."[38] In assessing this impulse, Salo Baron contended that "the new generation of historians outdid one another in passionate accounts of Israel's woes and sorrows."[39]

The scholar who may have outdone all others in this regard was Shimon Bernfeld, editor of the collection *Sefer ha-dema'ot* (The Book of Tears). The book was devoted, as the subtitle explains, to recounting the massacres, persecutions, and apostasies that befell Jews over the course of their history, including the Crusader violence, which Bernfeld described as nothing less than "the eternal foundation of Jewish history."[40] This three-volume work began to appear in Germany in 1923; it contained primary sources drawn from Jewish historical and liturgical literature, commencing with the persecutions inflicted on Jews by the Greek king Antiochus IV Epiphanes in the second century B.C.E. and extending up to the massacre in Uman in 1768.

The Galician-born Bernfeld was part of the stream of thousands of young east European Jews who made their way to Berlin at the turn of the twentieth century. It was there that he lived much of his adult life, producing works on Jewish history in both German and Hebrew. And it was there, in the early years of the Weimar Republic, that he became aware of the most recent tragedy of the Jews, the shocking pogroms that broke out in eastern Europe during and after the First World War that led to tens (and perhaps hundreds) of thousands of deaths. With that experience as the latest in a long martyrological chain, Bernfeld attached himself to an ancient tradition of Jewish sages who, as the Talmud (b. Shabbat 13a) memorably captured it, "cherished their troubles" (*hayu mehabevin et ha-tsarot*). Bernfeld observed in *Sefer ha-dema'ot* that "it was said about our forefathers that they cherished their troubles and, accordingly, recorded them as a memory." He continued, "Our predecessors wrote them down in order that the last generation should know, in order to fortify their hearts so that they could suffer and fight as the earlier generations suffered and fought. Not to strengthen the hand, but rather to strengthen the spirit of those who came after them. The stories of past woes are the future songs of consolation."[41]

This was the clinical embodiment of what Baron would call five years later "the lachrymose theory" of Jewish history.[42] True to form, Bernfeld completed the first volume of *Sefer ha-dema'ot* on Tisha b'Av, 1923, the fast day that marks the destruction of the two Holy Temples and other Jewish calamities. In opening that volume, he declared that the tales in his book "are truly the spine of Jewish history." In the intervening three years—a period in which Hitler attempted his Beer Hall Putsch in Munich, was imprisoned, and wrote *Mein Kampf*—Bernfeld finished two additional volumes. In the third volume, he summed up his labors by declaring that "the end of my book is not the end of the tragedy that we call Jewish history." Bernfeld did recognize that the modern age was different from its predecessors; the ghetto walls that once confined Jews had fallen, as had other restrictions placed on them. Nevertheless, hatred of the Jews "has grown in recent years and gains strength day by day."[43] Bernfeld's response, as a modern university-trained scholar, was strikingly similar to that of earlier chroniclers who recounted past tragedies as a means of fortification, sustenance, and consolation to Jews.

In confronting recent links in the chain of violence, modern Jewish historians have consoled their readers by pointing out that despite the ravages visited upon Jews, they were still standing after all was said and done. This record of endurance reduced even the most secular of historians to mystics of sorts. Simon Dubnow, who had already turned away from traditional observance by his bar mitzvah, became rhapsodic when discussing the survival of the Jews. Dubnow participated in a symposium on the topic in 1911 sponsored by the Hebrew journal *He-'atid* (The Future). On that occasion, he felt obliged to explain to fellow Jews how they would weather the storm of assimilation now confronting them. In an essay titled "The Secret of Survival—and the Law of Survival—of the Jewish People," he declared: "You imagine that there was never a period like this in Jewish history, a period of assimilation and apostasy. You're wrong. On many occasions, the destructiveness of Exile was felt—in Alexandria and Syria in the time of the Temple (despite the influence of the Judean center), in countries under the control of the Eastern Caliphate, in Arab [*sic*] and Christian Spain. None of this prevented the law of survival [of the Jews] from doing its work."[44]

Dubnow here consoled Jews through recourse to the lessons of the past, while at the same time cajoling them to recognize the secret of survival: acknowledgment of the national character of Jewry. It is instructive to juxtapose that message with Dubnow's words twelve years later, when he joined with the Russian-Jewish historian Elias Tcherikower to produce a collection of sources related to the widespread pogroms that broke out in 1919 in Ukraine and resulted in tens of thousands of Jewish deaths. The massive disruptions of the First World War had shifted Dubnow's focus from the longue durée of assimilation to the equally lengthy history of anti-Judaism. "Many peoples," Dubnow wrote in 1923, "have inscribed their names in the history of the millennial Jewish martyrology. But not many of them, indeed, none of them, have occupied as distinguished a place as the Ukrainian people." It is striking that Dubnow, well known for his criticism of Graetz's emphasis on the history of suffering, here speaks without reservation of a Jewish martyrology. Faced with the devastation of the pogroms, and armed with a sweeping command of Jewish history, he now saw before his eyes an interminable trail of destruction, which he cast in traditional terms, referring to "all the Pharaohs of Egypt and the past Hamans up to the collective Hamans of the recent periods." Rather than follow the ways of the nations of the world in their pursuit of bloodthirsty revenge, however, the Jews were different. They remained beholden to the biblical commandments to abstain from murder, theft, and adultery. "Our only revenge," Dubnow announced, "is immortalizing the slaughters in our history."[45]

It is interesting to compare Dubnow's postmortem conso-

lation, delivered while he was living in Berlin, to a more antic-
ipatory version forged a decade later in the same city. In 1933,
the department store magnate and book publisher Salmann
Schocken inaugurated at his new printing press a series of small
volumes written by leading Jewish scholars and artists of his day
(including S. Y. Agnon, Chaim Nachman Bialik, Martin Buber,
Heinrich Graetz, Franz Rosenzweig, and Gershom Scholem
among many others) or containing classical texts drawn from
the Jewish past. From the first publication until the last in 1938,
eighty-three volumes of the Schocken Bücherei series appeared,
covering a vast range of themes and prompting Ismar Schorsch
to marvel fifty years later at the "almost unbounded cultural
range and the speed at which it was produced."[46]

With the series, Salmann Schocken was attempting to capture and memorialize the extraordinary riches of "Jewish literature from all lands and times." It could then serve as an enduring testament to the vitality and creativity of that literary
culture. At the same time, the series was to provide a measure of
spiritual sustenance to German Jews during a period of rising
peril and narrowing cultural horizons. It is in that spirit that
Yitzhak Baer, the German-born historian in Jerusalem, published his 1936 valedictory to exile, *Galut*. And it is in that spirit
that Schocken placed as the first volume in the series a collection of sayings from Isaiah translated into German by Martin
Buber and Franz Rosenzweig, *Die Tröstung Israels: The Consolation of Israel*.[47]

THE PRAXIS OF HISTORICAL CONSOLATION

Dubnow's post-pogrom collection and the Schocken Bücherei
represent related, though distinct, forms of consolation: the former followed a familiar path by brandishing the survival of the
Jews after the fact; the latter provided a source of comfort in

medias res, through the praxis of historical writing itself. An interesting instance of the second form emerged in the vibrant Jewish community of Salonica in Greece in the interwar period. Devin E. Naar has excavated a cohort of scholars including Joseph Nehama, Isaac Emmanuel, and Michael Molho who, facing rising anti-Jewish agitation and economic crisis in the 1930s, "turned to the annals of their own past to provide comfort (*afalago*), consolation (*konorte*), and inspiration" as a means of boosting the morale of Salonican Jews. By recalling the glories of the past, they sought to encourage their fellow Jews to aspire "to return to 'our' previous heights."[48]

A similar impulse guided the Oyneg Shabbes project, which is surely one of the clearest instances of historical research in extremis ever recorded. The project brought together Jewish scholars and lay writers, religious and secular, socialist and nationalist, rich and poor, in the increasingly constricted conditions of the Warsaw Ghetto to chronicle what they and their coreligionists were undergoing between 1939 and 1942. We know a great deal more about the project due to Samuel D. Kassow's magisterial *Who Will Write Our History?* which brings to light the extraordinary labors of Emanuel Ringelblum, the Polish-Jewish historian who was the leader of the Oyneg Shabbes project.[49] Writing in late 1942, after three years of intensive labor, Ringelblum recalled that at the outset of the project *all* were called to the task of recording: "journalists, authors, teachers, community workers, young children, even children." The larger goal for which this assortment of laborers assembled was to preserve an accurate account of the murder of European Jewry for future generations. This was not cast as a partisan task. Ringelblum once averred to a colleague, "We have to regard ourselves as participants in a *universal* attempt to construct a solid structure of objective documentation that will work for the good of mankind."[50] It is astonishing to hear Ringelblum insist on upholding the values of universalism and objectivity while dwelling in the belly of the Nazi beast.[51]

In fact, the reader is moved by Ringelblum's unyielding devotion to history as a vital medium of truth. He and his colleagues harbored the hope that history would serve as an ultimate vindication of the triumph of good over evil. We are also struck by the organization, comprehensiveness, and balance of the Oyneg Shabbes circle, which proudly refused to portray all Poles or even all Germans as evil.[52] As a result of the thousands of documents left behind by the circle, we have a richly detailed and poignant record of daily life within the Warsaw Ghetto that serves as a fitting legacy to the compilers' industry and ingenuity.

But alongside this considerable achievement, the work of the Oyneg Shabbes group also provided a measure of escape from the enormous pressures of the day. Participants sought to gain distance from the grim world around them by undertaking a meticulous, multifaceted survey of ghetto life. The product was not merely a bequest to future generations. It was also a form of therapeutic self-consolation in its own right, providing participants with a sense of purpose, both at a daily and a more global level. Through its work of historical compilation, the Oyneg Shabbes circle also joined in what the Yiddish historian Mark Dworzecki was already calling in 1946 "spiritual resistance," a term that has come to embrace the wide range of cultural, religious, and social activities in which Jews engaged as they sought a measure of normality in the face of Nazi dehumanization.[53]

Dworzecki's concept captured the will to live of Jews in the most dire of circumstances, including the assumption of imminent death. Those committed to this form of resistance, including the members of the Oyneg Shabbes circle, engaged in a kind of self-consolation in medias res, utilizing the media of history and culture to remind themselves and their persecutors that they had not surrendered. We have also traced a lineage of chroniclers in this chapter who recalled past travails ex post facto as a form of consolation. At times, the chroniclers called attention to the cyclical nature of history, a pattern to which, they believed, the Jews were partly subject and which they frequently transcended. In both cases, these diverse groups of actors belong to a tradition of "interim Jewish hopes for the times before the end of Time."

By way of conclusion, I would like to mention a serious and underappreciated modern Jewish historian who grasped the underlying logic of studying and writing history as an act of consolation. The German-Jewish scholar Selma Stern conducted pioneering research on early-modern central European Jewish history, including on the interaction between the state and its Jews. Her most popular book was *The Court Jew*, written in 1950, nine years after she came to the United States with her husband, the ancient historian Eugen Täubler. Prompted by the recently concluded war to assess the Jews' place in history, Stern resorted to a cyclical view of history, though a positive version thereof, in which "everything dies in order that it may be reborn." The experience of the Court Jew, the classic liminal figure, embodied the ebbs and flows of Jewish history. "For time and again," she argued, "the Jew has helped prepare the way for a new era, only to find himself ground between the old forces which had outlived their day and the new which, with his help, were giving the world the promise of a better future."[54] Recognizing this pattern had its benefits, chief among which was solace. For, Stern concluded, "what one can understand one can endure."[55] Recognizing the travails of the past—and surviving them—was an important way of bearing the pain from them. Just as history was called upon to liberate, so too it has been called upon to console by demonstrating both the trials and the perdurance of the Jews.

3

History as Witness

Yidn, shraybt un farshraybt.
[Jews, write and record.]
SIMON DUBNOW, December 1941

Up to this point, we have followed two paths marked out by Jewish historians and frequented by their readers: liberation and consolation. In many cases, the historians I have discussed, most but not all of whom have been Jewish, have written in ways that traverse the boundary between history and memory. That is, they have aimed not merely to provide a factual reconstruction of past events but to use historical recollection to inspire, ground, and craft memory. Some may regard these functions as a distraction from, or even an abrogation of, what we might call the Thucydidean Code—the historian's commitment to produce "an exact knowledge of the past," as the ancient Greek formulated it. Thucydides stated that he set out to write history not "to win the applause of the moment, but as a possession for all time." This timeless quality toward which he strove could not tolerate an excess of distortion or subjectivity.[1]

At the same time, Thucydides believed that an accurate rendering of the past could serve as "an aid to the interpretation of the future." Indeed, this seems to represent a minimalist understanding of the historian's utility—the assembly of knowledge dispassionately gathered in order to enlighten future generations. It seems especially important to acknowledge and embrace this function in our current age, in which the study of history can be cast as an expendable luxury, especially when compared to the STEM disciplines (science, technology, engineering, and math). In fact, history is an essential, though oft-neglected, ingredient in informed civic engagement and policy debate.

Alongside this function, it is also important to remember the calling of the historian as a "physician of memory," to borrow the phrase of Eugen Rosenstock-Huessy repeated by Yosef Yerushalmi on several occasions. Often enough, the modern Jewish historian has paired a commitment to the methods of the guild with a desire to fortify the historical consciousness and remembrances of the collective.

This chapter will explore a version of this mission by tracing the ways in which history and the historian serve as *witnesses*. Admittedly, we do not think of history as the primary realm in which the witness operates. Religion makes a greater claim on the witness, who is called upon to affirm the truth claims of the faith. The stakes of religious witnessing have been high, as is evident in the close association between "witness" and the Greek word for "martyr," the latter of which was often used by early Christians interchangeably with the former.[2] Witnessing was, in that sense, a matter of life and death.

So too witnessing is a vital part of the process of legal adjudication. In biblical times, an obligation to come forward to testify to what one witnessed on pain of punishment had already been articulated (Lev. 5:1). Since that time, most systems of law practiced in the world have depended on witnessing, often requiring two eyewitnesses to corroborate (or discredit) each other's account. In related fashion, we note the way literature serves as a witness, especially in the wake of trauma or tragedy.[3] We might think here of the proliferation of fiction in the wake of the Holocaust, as author-survivors sought to give insight into an experience that verged on the unknowable. One of the most profound of this cohort of writers, Primo Levi, fused the literary and legal functions of the witness in his own writerly practice, as he averred in *The Reawakening:* "When describing the tragic world of Auschwitz, I have deliberately assumed the calm, sober language of the witness, neither the lamenting tones of the victim, nor the irate voice of someone who seeks revenge. I thought that my account would be all the more credible and useful the more it appeared objective and the less it sounded overly emotional; only in this way does a witness in matters of justice perform his task, which is that of preparing the ground for the judge."[4]

This plea for sobriety and objectivity calls to mind another Italian Jew, the historian Carlo Ginzburg, who reflected on the fate of the witness in the wake of the Holocaust in an important essay dedicated to Primo Levi. In "Just One Witness," published in a conference volume edited by Saul Friedlander, *Probing the Limits of Representation* (1992), Ginzburg undertakes to perform three interrelated functions: first, to juxtapose the legal tradition of relying on two witnesses for verification to the historian's practice of sufficing with one; second, to suggest that, despite their "different rules and different methodological foundations," law and history, following the eighteenth-century Jesuit Henri Griffet, in fact rest on a shared commitment to proof and truth; and third, to criticize scholars who abandon that commitment in favor of "skepticism and relativism" and thereby challenge the very possibility of historical veracity. As he makes abundantly clear, Ginzburg's chief target in this last regard is Hayden White, whose 1973 *Metahistory* is, to his mind, the locus classicus of historical skepticism. Ginzburg probes deeply, albeit not always persuasively, into White's intellectual biography to root this skepticism in the subjectivist stance of the Italian fascist philosopher Giovanni Gentile. He traces this rather ignominious historical genealogy in order to reveal the high moral cost of attacks on historical truth.[5]

In his battle against "the lazily radical form of skepticism," Ginzburg imagines the historian as a particularly qualified and effective agent of witnessing. He exemplified this point in a small, curious volume he wrote in Italian around the same time as "Just One Witness" that appeared in English eight years later as *The Judge and the Historian* (1999).[6] The book was an extended brief in defense of his friend Adriano Sofri, who was accused of murdering an Italian policeman in 1972 while a member of an underground leftist cell. Ginzburg maintained absolute certainty in Sofri's innocence and set out to expose the "miscarriage of justice" that led to his conviction in 1990. Over the course of his inquiry, he discovered divergences between historians and judges in how they used sources, understood facts, and made use of contexts.[7] And yet, Ginzburg here and elsewhere insisted that the meticulous sifting of evidence, along with careful argumentation, could serve as a counterweight to efforts to blur the boundary between fact and fiction.

In productive tension with Ginzburg stands the late Yale legal scholar Robert Cover. Cover did not directly address the function of the witness. Instead, he discussed in a widely cited *Harvard Law Review* article, "Nomos and Narrative" (1983–1984), the potential inhering in law not only to achieve clarity about what was but also to serve as "a bridge linking a concept of a reality to an imagined alternative."[8] Cover elaborated on this point in his 1985 article "The Folktales of Justice," in which he outlined a position that he defined as "very close to a classical anarchist one." That is, Cover considered the potential of judges to use the law to curb and "call to account" kings who might overstep their power. The moral demand to deliver justice is tempered by fear of retribution, leading to a "necessarily difficult tightrope act that judges must perform." Cover also discusses another important balancing act in the work of law: that between myth and history. Myth, he wrote with echoes of R. G. Collingwood, is what "we create and choose to remember in order to *reenact*." History, by contrast, is "a counter-move bringing us back to reality, requiring that we test the aspiration objectively and prudentially." The two interact in essential ways: myth promotes the aspirational vision of human beings for a better society, whereas history disrupts and challenges the vision by recalling how difficult fulfillment of the quest will be. Working hand in glove, myths "supply *purpose* for history."[9]

What is the point of my juxtaposing two such diverse scholars as Carlo Ginzburg and Robert Cover? Both, it must be noted, were keenly interested in the interrelationship of law and history—and the place of narrative in each. Ginzburg, for his part, is intent on upholding the possibility of evidence-based narrative to describe that which is *real* through an emphasis on the criterion of proof. Cover, on the other hand, focused on the *constructive* potential of an interpretive legal narrative to build a bridge to the *ideal*. The two eminent scholars push to the fore a set of tensions—between history and law, history and memory, the real and the ideal, traditional and redemptive visions—that play an animating role in the labors of the historian in general, and as witness, in particular.

From Textual to Legal Witnessing

The relationship between history and witnessing operates at various levels. First, history, in a metaphorical sense, provides witness to certain events that unfold over its course. Second, the evidentiary base of history depends, to a great extent, on witnesses, in both oral and written form. Third, and of most direct interest to this chapter, historians have been called upon to serve as actual witnesses in trials. In her study of the relationship between survivor testimony and collective memory after the Holocaust, the French scholar Annette Wieviorka homed in on the central role of historians, who "were the first to recognize, in the midst of the genocide, the urgent necessity of bearing witness so that history could one day be written." After the war, they acted on this recognition by offering testimony in Holocaust-related trials, thereby contributing to what Wieviorka described as "the era of the witness."[10] In doing so, they were crafting a picture of the past with an eye to those who might not have experienced or even lived during the events. They were thus crafting memory for a future generation.

Well before the advent of the "era of the witness," historians were engaged in various forms of witnessing. We return to the familiar figure Simon Dubnow, who assumed the role of historical witness on numerous occasions, albeit not in the courtroom but rather in print form. In the aftermath of the Kishinev pogroms of 1903 in which scores of Jews were brutally murdered in southern Russia, he joined forces with the Hebrew poet Chaim Nachman Bialik to collect evidence, including firsthand accounts, of the violence. He published a number of articles about the pogrom based on Bialik's onsite reports, but he did not realize his grander plan of editing a three-volume compendium of primary sources with an overarching narrative. Still, the kernel of the idea to generate a collection of sources that provided textual witness to persecutions under the rubric of *khurbn-forshung* (research of a major destruction) was born out of this crisis.[11]

As we saw in the previous chapter, Dubnow collaborated twenty years later with a new partner, Elias Tcherikower, to chronicle the massive loss of life and destruction in the anti-Jewish pogroms in Ukraine during and especially after the First World War. Although the original design called for a seven-volume series under the rubric of the Eastern (European) Jewish Historical Archive, Tcherikower and Dubnow collaborated on a single volume of textual witnessing, divided between narrative and sources, that appeared in 1923 as *Anṭisemiṭism un pogromen in Uḳraine, 1917–1918.* This text belonged to a larger spate of documentary projects, which extended from Europe to the United States, chronicling the pogroms. It was, as the historian Alexandra Garbarini notes, the era of the documentary collection, one in which "victim testimony and historical scholarship now became a way to bring the perpetrators of mass atrocity to justice."[12]

Simon Dubnow's grandest act—and ultimate sacrifice—as witness came a little less than twenty years after that, as he faced death in 1941. Eight years earlier, he had left Berlin, where he had been for over a decade, for Riga, Latvia, intent on realizing his ideal of Jewish national autonomy in his native eastern Europe. His curious decision to head to Riga, rather than Palestine or America, proved deadly. In July 1941, the German army occupied Latvia and began to round up the local Jewish population. In October, Nazi forces placed Dubnow and his fellow Jews in a ghetto in Riga. They began liquidations the next month. Dubnow, who was already in an infirm state at eighty-one years of age, was killed on 8 December in the massacre of Jews that took place in the Rumbula forest.

Multiple accounts of his death exist. According to one, he was shot in the back of the head by a drunken Latvian soldier. In another he was killed by a German soldier who had been a student of his when he taught in Heidelberg. A variant of that account reports that this former student, Johann Siebert, would boast to Dubnow about the number of Jews that had been liquidated each day, to which Dubnow, who was working without cease, would retort, "I will record it all."[13] Even more poignant and better known are the final words Dubnow was said to have uttered as he walked to his death: "Yidn, shraybt un farshraybt"—"Jews, write and record."[14]

This charge has become a legend—and a particularly fitting one given Dubnow's vocation. Indeed, it stands as a powerful credo for the modern Jewish historian, who has answered the call to record the past as a shield against indifference and a monument to memory. It was the same impulse that informed the Oyneg Shabbes project, perhaps the greatest example of textual witnessing in modern Jewish history. Not only did Emanuel Ringelblum encourage his colleagues to "write and record" all that transpired in the Warsaw Ghetto; he was inspired by the earlier Dubnow-Tcherikower collection project, which was seen not merely as an assembly of historical details but as a repository of memory and a plea for justice.[15]

Ringelblum, Dubnow, and Tcherikower were important contributors to this era of textual witnessing, though only the last figure, Tcherikower, had the opportunity to translate his historical and documentary expertise into courtroom testimony when he was called to testify at a trial in 1927. Even before that time, the modern scholar had assumed the role of witness in courtrooms, often under the shadow of antisemitism.[16] One early case was that of the prominent late-nineteenth-century philosopher (though not historian) Hermann Cohen, who provided testimony at a trial in 1888 at which a local teacher was accused of slandering Judaism. Although the teacher was technically the defendant, it was really the Talmud, as the historian Ulrich Sieg notes, that was on trial. As a prosecution witness, Cohen was asked to offer an expert opinion on the extent to which the Talmud was binding for Jews and whether it permitted Jews to defraud non-Jews. He squared off against the defense team's main witness, the Göttingen orientalist and antisemite Paul de Lagarde, who submitted written testimony.[17] After weighing the two "expert" accounts and the defendant's own testimony, the judges ruled against the defendant and Lagarde and in favor of Cohen's position.

With the turn of the nineteenth to the twentieth century, the task of the scholar-witness shifted from the defense of Judaism to the prosecution of perpetrators.[18] This, of course, marked a far more consequential shift from an age of intense anti-Jewish rhetoric to one of mass violence, commencing with Kishinev, progressing to the Ukrainian pogroms, and culminating in the Holocaust.

THE HISTORIAN TAKES THE STAND

It is important to recall that historians assume a variety of tasks in the legal sphere. They are called upon to provide contextual backdrop to assist in preparing a case, help craft strategy, and write influential friend-of-the-court briefs. Magda Teter has chronicled a number of notable cases in American legal history such as John Hope Franklin's influential collaboration with Thurgood Marshall in the run-up to the *Brown v. Board of Education* desegregation case of 1954. She also notes the prominent role of historians such as Nancy Cott, Michael Grossberg, and George Chauncey in writing persuasive amicus briefs in cases involving marriage equality and equal rights for members of the lesbian-gay-bisexual-transgender community.[19]

In these various ways, history, through the medium of the historian, asserts itself in the domain of law. And yet the most visible and demonstrative encounter between history and law may well occur when the historian takes the stand as expert witness. One of the most significant affirmations of this point came in the *EEOC v. Sears* trial of the 1970s and 1980s. The case pitted two distinguished scholars of women's history, Rosalind Rosenberg and Alice Kessler-Harris, on either side of the claim that the Sears department store chain discriminated against women in employment and pay. Apart from the legal merits of the case, the two disagreed over the function of history. In recalling her decision to testify, Rosenberg, who was sharply criticized by many feminist and women's historians, insisted that "scholars must not subordinate their scholarship to their politics even if their scholarship appears to be heading in a politically dangerous direction." Kessler-Harris, by contrast, adopted a perspective that acknowledged the difficulty of complete value-neutrality in a case such as this: "You would not lie in your testimony, but you also would not say or write something as a historian solely to hurt a group of people."[20]

In the precincts of Jewish history, historians have been called on to serve as witnesses in cases involving claims of mass violence. The twentieth-century tradition begins with Elias Tcherikower, who testified at the trial of Sholem Schwarzbard in 1927. Schwarzbard was the Bessarabian-born Jewish anarchist who was so distraught by the deaths of tens of thousands of Jews in Ukraine, including fifteen members of his own family, that he assassinated in May 1926 Symon Petliura, the Ukrainian nationalist leader whom he held responsible for the deaths. Following the murder, a number of Jewish historians, including Dubnow and Tcherikower, contributed to Schwarzbard's defense by collecting and sharing evidence intended to prove Petliura's central role in the pogroms.[21] Tcherikower was, in all probability, the leading expert in the world on the 1919 pogrom, and thus was an obvious choice for Schwarzbard's lawyer, the French Jew Henry Torrès, to choose as chief historical witness. The defense strategy was to refocus the trial from the assassination in Paris to the murderous destruction in Ukraine. Tcherikower drew on his wide-ranging knowledge and massive trove of documents in his testimony to conclude that "responsibility for the pogroms which were accomplished in the Ukraine falls upon Petlura."[22] With his testimony as a key factor in Torrès's strategy, the jury took all of fifteen minutes of deliberation to acquit Schwarzbard.

Tcherikower thus stands as a prototype of the twentieth-century historical witness.[23] Given his prominent role in a trial dealing with anti-Jewish atrocities, one might have expected to see Jewish historians widely represented in what has been called "the greatest history seminar ever held in the history of the world"—namely, the Nuremberg trials of 1945–1946, at which the Allies sought to bring Nazi war criminals to justice.[24] Jewish organizations, led by the Institute of Jewish Affairs of the World Jewish Congress, whose head was the legal scholar and historian Jacob Robinson, agitated for strong Jewish representation to give an overarching view of the scale of destruction at Nuremberg.[25] Robinson made this point clear in a meeting on 12 June 1945 with U.S. Supreme Court Justice Robert H. Jackson, who served as chief American prosecutor at Nuremburg. Jackson thought that the most effective person to present "the total picture of the Holocaust" was not a historian, but the renowned Zionist leader Chaim Weizmann.[26] Jackson's plan was never realized owing to the fears of the British team about granting too large a stage to a Zionist leader in 1945, given the ongoing turmoil in Palestine. But beyond the prospect of Weizmann as a witness, the Nuremberg prosecutors doubted the wisdom of centering their case around the testimony of Jews. As Donald Bloxham has pointed out, they "suspected [Jewish testimony] as being somehow biased, and more so than that of other groups."[27] This was the source of great disappointment to Jacob Robinson and the Institute for Jewish Affairs. Nonetheless, Robinson and his fellow researchers offered indispensable assistance to Justice Jackson and his team, compiling a thicket of memoranda, reports, profiles of Nazi defendants, and statistical figures. Robinson described the work of his Institute team as "extraordinary," which only pointed up the irony he noted regarding the Allied prosecution team: "We, those who are competent, are on the outside, and those who are on the inside are incompetent."[28]

If Jewish historians did not play a prominent role as witnesses at Nuremberg, they did have a key background part in convicting Nazi war criminals, as well as in the longer-term goal of crafting a compelling didactic history of the Holocaust. Serving along with Robinson was Philip Friedman, an eminent yet oft-forgotten Polish-Jewish historian and survivor who contributed to the preparation of the Nuremberg cases. Friedman was one of a small cohort of survivor-historians writing in Yiddish during and immediately after the war—others included Rachel (Rokhl) Auerbach, Mark Dworzecki, Yosef Kermish, and Isaiah Trunk—who undertook remarkable and prescient research into the Holocaust.[29] We have also gained a fuller picture in recent years of the workings of two sets of Jewish institutions that made extensive use of history in the immediate postwar period of extraterritorial transitional justice for Jews: historical commissions staffed by survivors in displaced persons camps and European countries, and Jewish honor courts set up to determine the degree to which Jews collaborated with the Nazis.[30]

History in the hands of these individuals and groups not only served as witness to the ruins of European Jewish life, it also reflected their deep passion to pursue justice and demand accountability. It was later, following the Nuremberg proceedings (which lasted until 1949), that historians appeared as witnesses in courtrooms, offering both broad context and specific detail with the dispassionate mien of the expert. Not only were they motivated to testify by the unprecedented nature of the Nazi genocidal campaign, which Jean-François Lyotard likened to an earthquake that "destroys not only lives, buildings, and objects but also the instruments used to measure earthquakes."[31] They also had at their disposal a vast and detailed repository of incriminating historical documents produced by the Nazis themselves. Accordingly, German historians began to testify as expert witnesses in court cases against Nazi war criminals in the late

1950s and early 1960s. In Ulm, Germany, for example, the historian Helmut Krausnick testified in 1958 against ten members of an Einsatzgruppen unit accused of killing thousands of Jews in Lithuania. Krausnick was also one of four historians—the others were Martin Broszat, Hans Buchheim, and Hans-Adolf Jacobsen—who played a key role in the prosecution in Frankfurt in 1963 of twenty-two S.S. Auschwitz functionaries.[32]

It was in this same period that a scholar of Jewish history made a widely publicized appearance at the trial of an accused war criminal. Salo W. Baron was called to the stand as the expert historical witness in the trial of S.S. officer Adolf Eichmann in Jerusalem in 1961. Baron's selection for this task, for all of his prominence, was far from a foregone conclusion. In the highly unusual deliberations that preceded the trial, in which the leading political officials of the State of Israeli were involved, Prime Minister David Ben-Gurion challenged the wisdom of bringing Baron in from New York. He doubted Baron's Zionist bona fides and expressed a strong preference for having Zalman Shazar (later president of Israel) assume the role. Part of Ben-Gurion's reluctance may have stemmed from Baron's well-known resistance to the "lachrymose" view of Jewish history as a long series of persecutions. In fact, the situation was more complicated, since Baron did *not* hold to a uniformly rosy view of the modern age in Jewish history.[33] But neither did he possess the requisite pessimism about the prospects for diaspora life that was a foundation of the Zionist worldview of Ben-Gurion and the Israeli attorney general and chief Eichmann prosecutor, Gideon Hausner.[34]

Nonetheless, it was Baron whom Israeli Justice Minister Pinchas Rosen instructed the consul-general in New York, Benjamin Eliav, to invite to testify in late December 1960. Rosen's memo to Eliav contained a detailed charge that reflected Hausner's desires. The Columbia historian was to offer in his testimony "a general description of the status of European Jewry on the eve of the Catastrophe, its importance, and national as well as cultural quality, a general description of the human and national potential contained in it, as well as a description of the remnants of the culture which remained after the Catastrophe when the holocaust ended." The chief point, Rosen added with passing reference to a classic Zionist tenet, was to affirm that "there had existed a dispersion [i.e., the Diaspora] in possession of great values—which now no longer exists."[35]

With wide-ranging and often conflicting expectations—not to mention, pressure—placed on him, Baron took the stand on 24 April 1961. In his accented Galician Hebrew, for which he apologized at the outset, Baron delivered a long survey that touched on the demographic, economic, geographic, educational, cultural, and intellectual status of Jews before the war. A key part of his task was what is now deemed a rather intuitive and commonplace assumption among scholars: that in order to grasp the enormity of the destruction of the Shoah, it is necessary to take stock of the full range of Jewish cultural vitality prior to the war.[36] This is precisely what Ben-Gurion wanted of Baron, as he stated in a meeting two weeks before his testimony: "It is important to make clear to our youth (and also to the world) the magnitude of the qualitative loss, resulting from the extermination of Six Million [Jews], and therefore [we must describe] the spiritual character of the Jewry that was exterminated." And it was on this point that Gideon Hausner and presiding judge Moshe Landau sought to draw out Baron. At times the exchange between witness and judge became exceedingly mundane, as, for example, when Baron was describing the vast array of Jewish newspapers published in Europe in the 1930s. He counted 96 in France, 21 in Holland, 16 in Austria, 21 in Hungary, 54 in Romania, 15 in Lithuania, and 113 in Germany. After listing these figures, Baron was asked by a perhaps inattentive Judge Landau: "Are you referring to periodicals?" Baron responded affirmatively, before going on to mention 35 daily Jewish papers in Poland, along with 132 weeklies.[37]

As Hanna Yablonka has noted, the fear that Baron's lengthy recitation would be boring and ineffective concerned some of those intimately involved in the preparation for the trial, including Jacob Robinson, who had moved to Israel after his work on the Nuremberg trials and was now Hausner's chief historical adviser. In fact, Baron's overall mission, as crafted by Ben-Gurion, Hausner, and Robinson, was virtually impossible to fulfill. He was called upon to be comprehensive and thorough but at the same time sharp and engaging. He was asked to describe the grand achievements of diaspora life, while adding credence to a linear narrative that culminated in its destruction. And he was supposed to be both exacting in detail and yet lapidary in assessing the full course of Jewish history.

At various points in his testimony, even the sober-minded Baron lapsed into a kind of mystical reverie (an occupational hazard, it seems, of Jewish macrohistorians who must explain the Jews' survival, as Dubnow sought to do earlier). When recalling some of the towering figures of modern Jewish and Zionist history—Albert Einstein, Chaim Nachman Bialik, Chaim Weizmann, and David Ben-Gurion—he invoked the traditional belief in the Lamed-Vov Tsadikim, the thirty-six righteous Jews on whose existence the world rested. "I found in my lifetime," he continued, "more than 36 righteous men, exceptional Jews, in fact, abounding in their holy purity, both in the religious sense and the secular sense, who were prepared to sacrifice themselves for the common benefit." This statement prompted Judge Landau to ask if these figures were hidden, to which Baron responded: "They are hidden. They are unknown."[38]

More commonly, Baron made recourse not to mystical or celestial but rather to terrestrial explanations, even when analyzing what he saw as unique aspects of Jewish history. For example, in reflecting on the disproportionate impact of Jews on world culture, he noted their need and ability "to find new openings for themselves," to create new paths when old ones were no longer available to them. Baron explained this adaptive mechanism through use of a curious, though not altogether surprising (given the preparation he had received), term: *halutziut,* the Hebrew word for "pioneering" associated with the early socialist Zionist settlers. "This pioneering spirit, this Halutziut," Baron observed, "was a constant feature in the history of the Jews, both in economics and in social affairs, and also, especially in culture, from the days of the Babylonian exile to the present day."[39]

The struggle to resist metaphysical leaps in spanning the entirety of Jewish history was not only an inner battle. At the conclusion of his testimony, Baron also had to parry the thrusts of Eichmann's German defense lawyer, Robert Servatius, who tried to insist that the long history of antisemitism was an unbroken chain motivated by irrational forces beyond the free will of individuals. Baron rooted his response to Servatius in mundane terms. He not only insisted on the agency of individuals such as Eichmann in history; he challenged the insinuation that an enduring religious stigma against the Jews existed. Treatment of Jews under the Nazis was very different from treatment of the Jews prior to the modern age. Consistent with the view announced in "Ghetto and Emancipation," Baron held that "there was practically no violence with bloodshed" against Jews in the ancient and medieval periods.[40] By contrast, he had earlier declared that "the Nazi movement not only did not turn the clock back . . . it brought to the world new elements which had no precedent but which were distinct from the whole history of anti-Semitism of two thousand years and more."[41]

This was not the answer that Servatius was seeking. Nor did

Baron deliver the exact answers for which Ben-Gurion and Robinson were looking. Both sharply criticized Baron's performance as ineffective and error-riddled. Ben-Gurion, for his part, confided to a small group in November 1961, "He embarrassed us. He spoke with me, and I knew at once that we had failed miserably."[42] No doubt, Baron's anti-lachrymose view of the distant past did not comport with Ben-Gurion's classic Zionist vision of "negating the Diaspora." Nor, for that matter, did Baron's style win universal praise among observers. Various international journalists, as Yablonka notes, questioned the efficacy of his presentation. But by no means was there universal condemnation. A number of Israeli newspapers gave an uncritical description of Baron, as did the *New York Times* under the heading "Eichmann Court Hears Historian," adjacent to which was a lengthy profile, "Top Jewish Historian: Salo Wittmayer Baron."[43]

Navigating between the highly scripted demands of his Israeli handlers and his own professional judgment was a difficult, if not impossible, task. Equally challenging was the need to strike a balance between sweeping and granular approaches, between the longue durée of Jewish history and antisemitism and the particularities of interwar Jewish life and Nazi efforts to extinguish it. In light of these challenges, Baron did more than a credible job in his several hours of testimony, though it may not have risen, at least in rhetorical terms, to the "masterly summation" that his biographer claimed.[44]

Regardless of how we assess his performance, two distinct, though interrelated, points emerge from the Eichmann trial: first, Baron pushed—or was prompted to push—the function of the Jewish historian well beyond the limited ambit of the academy and into the public sphere. In fact, the primary audience to whom he was speaking was not the panel of judges before him but the wider public, as his handlers knew well in aspiring for a lively and compelling presentation. Baron was also testifying for posterity, to establish a definitive account of the past that would serve as an anchor for the memory of future generations. These functions led to a second point, articulated by Hannah Arendt; namely, that "it was history that, as far as the prosecution was concerned, stood in the center of the trial."[45] Arendt insisted in *Eichmann in Jerusalem* that this was not an effective or sincere use of history; rather, it was an abuse of history for the purposes of a staged show trial.[46] And although she may have misjudged the banality of Eichmann's evil, as Bettina Stangneth has recently argued, she is on target in describing the staged quality of the trial.[47]

But did its theatricality undermine the value of the trial altogether? In his study of political trials in *The Memory of Judgment,* Lawrence Douglas addresses the category of "didactic history." For Douglas, when political trials have failed, "it was not the pursuit of didactic history that ultimately eroded the legal integrity of the proceeding conventionally conceived; rather it was the strenuous efforts to secure formal legal integrity that often led to a failure fully to do justice to traumatic history."[48] There can be no doubt that Ben-Gurion, Hausner, and Robinson had in mind to construct not merely a solid factual trial, but to set in place what Douglas called a "heroic memory" of the Holocaust in which an ineradicable boundary would mark off virtue and criminality.[49] With less overt and developed ideological intentions, Baron joined in that task and contributed his share through the professional medium of history. Sadly, mass murder did not cease after the Holocaust. It has recurred on varying scales in Cambodia, Rwanda, Darfur, the Congo, and Bosnia among others (and, of course, it surfaced earlier in the Armenian genocide of 1915). And yet, it is in confronting the criminal legacy of the Holocaust that historians—and history—have most directly assumed center stage in seeking justice and planting seeds of memory.

The "Judicialization of History" and
the Pursuit of Memory

Although notably preceded by Elias Tcherikower, Baron was the most famous example of a twentieth-century Jewish historian to take the stand at a legal trial. He lent new visibility to this public function of the historian. But he was hardly the last. From the late 1980s on, historians were called upon to testify in an expanding range of trials involving suspected Nazi war criminals and Holocaust deniers in Europe, Israel, and North America. Set against the rise of ominous new voices of denial and the fear of the passing of the survivor generation, these trials sought to establish an indelible memory of the Holocaust.

This is the context in which another distinguished Jewish historian took the stand in Lyon, France, in 1987, when Léon Poliakov, the prolific Russian-born French historian of antisemitism (who also served as an aide to the French team at Nuremberg), was called to testify at the trial of S.S. officer Klaus Barbie. Poliakov recalls that he had a grander mission than simply establishing Barbie's guilt. He also wanted to offer a definitive refutation of Holocaust denial and make a larger historical point: namely, that Hitler had in mind to undertake mass euthanasia beyond the Jewish population. Poliakov hoped that his testimony would reverberate beyond the witness stand into the popular media so as to leave a lasting imprint on future generations.[50]

It is important to note that not every historian feels comfortable with this kind of role. For example, Henri Rousso, the scholar of Vichy France, refused to participate in the trial of the accused war criminal Maurice Papon in 1997–1998. He de-

History as Witness / 92

clared unequivocally: "I believe that historians cannot be 'witnesses' and that a role as 'expert witness' rather poorly suits the rules and objectives of a court trial. It is one thing to try to understand history in the context of a research project or course lesson, with the intellectual freedom that such activities presuppose; it is quite another to try to do so under oath when an individual's fate hangs in the balance."[51] Rousso continued, "I very much fear that my 'testimony' is only a pretext for an instrumentalization of scientific research and historical interpretations." And to what end might "instrumentalization" lead? It could lead to what Hannah Arendt feared the Eichmann trial was conceived as, a concern echoed more recently by the historian Ian Buruma, who wrote: "When the court of law is used for history lessons, then the risk of show trials cannot be far off."[52]

Other historians felt differently about the function of historical witnessing and agreed to testify at the Papon trial in October 1997 in Bordeaux—in fact, on behalf of both the prosecution and the defense. The most notable of the scholar-witnesses was the Columbia historian Robert O. Paxton, whose *Vichy France: Old Guard and New Order* (1972) demolished previous views of the subservience of the Vichy regime toward France's Nazi occupiers. Paxton recognized that the Papon trial was intended to advance a pedagogical mission by demonstrating "how the Vichy regime fits into French history." While this mission was not fully realized, he maintained nonetheless that "all the pious clichés about wartime France were shredded in the gritty specificities revealed in the Bordeaux courtroom." Paxton also reflected on a distinctive feature of historical witnessing in an interview six months after testifying: "Historians don't decide the guilt or innocence of an individual with respect to the penal code. Historians are trying to understand the past, to make the past intelligible. But you certainly do judge—this person did well, that person didn't do well."[53]

It is this slippage of function from witness to judge that discourages some historians, such as Rousso, from testifying in trials and, more broadly, from participating in what the British historian Richard Evans has called the "judicialization of history." In contrast to Rousso, Evans *did* participate in a trial, serving as an expert for the defense of the American historian Deborah Lipstadt, who was accused of libel by British scholar David Irving whom she described as a Holocaust denier in *Denying the Holocaust: The Growing Assault on Truth and Memory* (1994). Evans recalls the instructions he received from Lipstadt's legal counsel, the British solicitor Anthony Julius, when approached about assisting in her defense in 1998. "Expert witnesses," he recalled, "were not there to plead a case. They were there to help the court in technical and specialized matters." Above all, the evidence they presented "had to be as truthful and objective as possible."[54] The insistence on precise details and exacting analysis of sources informed the "dream team" of experts that Julius brought together for the London trial, each of whom was a renowned scholar of the Second World War and the Holocaust: Evans, Christopher Browning, Peter Longerich, and Robert Jan van Pelt.[55] At the same time, these four were in the employ of the defense, and their goal was to uphold Deborah Lipstadt's claims that David Irving had repeatedly falsified the historical record in his dozens of books on the history of Germany during the war.

This case raised considerable apprehension among Holocaust survivors, academic researchers, and the general public that the Holocaust—and, as in the title of Deborah Lipstadt's subsequent book about the case, history itself—were on trial. Once again, a fear sunk in that the imminent passing of the last generation of eyewitnesses would open up the gates of Holocaust denial or falsification. This prospect exposed both the fragility and the strength of history. Could such an established fact as the Holocaust, which had generated a massive and seemingly irrefutable body of evidence, become an open question a mere fifty years after the events in question? Does the variable nature of historical interpretation destabilize the evidentiary foundation on which our notion of truth is placed? This was not the belief of the Lipstadt defense team, upon which the burden of proof rested per English libel laws. The defense attempted to demonstrate to the court that David Irving's work was rife with falsifications, inaccuracies, and errors, willfully driven by an antisemitic and racist ideology.

That claim was affirmed in decisive fashion by Judge Charles Gray on 11 April 2000. Gray recognized that "historians are human" and invariably "make mistakes, misread and misconstrue documents and overlook material evidence."[56] But he asserted without equivocation that "Irving's treatment of the historical evidence is so perverse and egregious that it is difficult to accept that it is inadvertence on his part. . . . He has deliberately skewed the evidence to bring it in line with his political beliefs."[57]

Despite Irving's efforts to salvage some vestige of honor after the trial, Gray's verdict in support of Lipstadt left little room for maneuver. Press and broader public reactions were overwhelmingly supportive of the decision. Both Lipstadt and Evans, for their part, wrote books about the trial, the final outcome of which they regarded as a powerful victory for history. For Evans, it was the integrity of the historian's vocation that was safeguarded. Several years earlier, he had published *In Defence of History* (1997) in order to contend with the challenge of postmodern theory to his field, dismissing some of its devotees as "intellectual barbarians at the disciplinary gate" while insisting that not all its claims should be met with mere ridicule. A similar approach informed his work on the Irving trial and the book he wrote about it, *Lying About Hitler*. He began by acknowledging perennial questions about the objectivity of history—about whether we can ever *know* the past in light of our personal and political proclivities. He admitted that all historians bring to their work some measure of personal investment. Evans even suggested that "in many ways Lipstadt seems as politically committed to her cause as Irving was to his." And yet, "The real test of a serious historian was the extent to which he or she was willing or able to subordinate political belief to the demands of historical research." In his judgment, Lipstadt met the standard, whereas Irving failed it dreadfully. The overall result of the case, he determined, was "a victory for history, for historical truth and historical scholarship."[58]

Lipstadt's own account made clear that she was fighting not only or primarily for the historian's craft but also on behalf of the victims and survivors of the Holocaust and against "the attempt to ravage their history and memory."[59] Although Evans asserted that Lipstadt "did not think that memory had won" in the trial, it is unclear if that position holds. Keenly attuned to the passage of time—and of the survivor cohort from the world—Lipstadt felt a sense of urgency in reinforcing "the history and memory" of the Holocaust. Accordingly, she sought both to prevent the history of the Holocaust from slipping into a state of interpretive indeterminacy *and* to assure that future generations built a firm edifice to remember the attempted genocide of European Jews.[60]

These differences in emphasis were slight compared to the shared goal Evans and Lipstadt had in beating back Irving's challenge—and to the sense of relief and elation they felt at trial's end. And yet, the differences between them help us identify a spectrum of positions regarding the role of the historian as witness. On one end is the view of Henri Rousso, who believes that the task of the historian is fundamentally unsuited to the legal process. "Be it as judge, prosecutor or advocate," Rousso wrote in *The Haunting Past,* "historians are no longer in their proper element once they don courtroom robes." Particularly unnerving to Rousso was the tendency of the historian to serve as an "agitator of collective memory." He drew a bright-line distinction between history and memory, the former depending first and foremost on factual accuracy and the latter on a more subjective "moralism."[61]

At the other end of the spectrum is the view of Lawrence Douglas, for whom history and memory are not antipodes but rather fluid and entwined domains. His analysis of Holocaust-related trials in *The Memory of Judgment* leads him to identify their multiple functions: "to clarify the historical record, define the terms of responsible memory, and make visible the efficacy of the rule of law." On this view, history, unmoored from its task as fact-finder alone, has the potential to foster both a "heroic memory" and the cause of justice.[62]

Richard Evans and Deborah Lipstadt stand between these two poles, but in somewhat different positions. Evans accepts the call to serve as an expert witness, but eschews the judge's task of rendering definitive judgment. Rather, history, to his mind, functions as an evidentiary aid to those called upon to deliver a verdict. In conceiving of his own sense of mission, he is adamant in insisting that the boundary between factual history and subjective memory must be maintained. Meanwhile, Lipstadt, who was not called to the stand herself but benefited greatly from historical witnesses, shares Evans's view that their chosen profession has the singular capacity to refute those who "distort, falsify, and pervert the historical record." The chief threat, she argued earlier in *Denying the Holocaust,* may not come from outright denial of the Holocaust, which defies all credulity, but rather from a relativistic stance that credits all interpretations of the past as equally valid. In the hands of deceitful Holocaust revisionists, she wrote, such a stance points up "the fragility of memory, truth, reason, and history." The task of the historian, then, must be not only to shore up history, as Evans imagines it, but also to lay a solid building block of memory for the future. The deep sense of obligation that Lipstadt feels to this task is epitomized by the concluding line of *Denying the Holocaust:* "The still, small voices of millions cry out to us from the ground demanding that we do no less."[63]

The Historian Between Remembering and Forgetting

Richard Evans and Deborah Lipstadt represent related though distinct sensibilities regarding the historian's function as witness and fortifier of memory. These sensibilities suggest to us that the stakes of historical recollection—and the historian's labor—are especially high in confronting the Holocaust. What must be remembered? What lessons are to be learned?

These questions have stimulated an impassioned debate among recent thinkers. They are responding to the growing tension between the rapid pace of change in our twenty-first-century cyber universe, in which there is a new headline or tragedy in every hourly turn of the news cycle, and the need to remember traumatic events and tragedies, which occur with unsettling frequency in our time. In one of the most direct engagements, the writer and reporter David Rieff argues forcefully in *In Praise of Forgetting* that collective remembrance is decidedly unstable, often ineffective, and full of the potential to lead to myopic chauvinism. He deals in considerable detail with the Jewish impulse to remember, as well as with Yosef Yerushalmi's *Zakhor*. Tacking back and forth between the virtues and dangers of forgetting, he concludes that "remembrance, however important a role it may and often does play in the life of groups, and whatever moral and ethical demands it not only responds to but often can fulfill, carries with it political and social risks that at times also have an existential character." Rieff suggests that even the canonical post-Holocaust mantra "Never Again" could fall prey to these risks.[1]

Two historians with distinctive angles on the Holocaust have recently offered strikingly different responses to the question of what can be learned from history in general and the Holocaust in particular. The Toronto historian Michael Marrus provides valedictory wisdom as an elder statesman of Holocaust research in questioning our ability to derive any single coherent or universal lesson from the study of the Shoah. "There are many purported lessons out there," he asserts, "and they cannot all have the same transcendent significance or validity." History, he continues, "does not speak to the present with so clear an admonitory voice."[2]

By contrast, Timothy Snyder, author of a number of major works on eastern European history, including two volumes that challenge our understanding of the Holocaust, concludes *Black Earth* by insisting that the history of the Holocaust must be recorded in order to be understood, and "it must be understood so that its like can be prevented in the future."[3] Moving from the abstract to the concrete, as well as from the past to the present, Snyder urges us to recognize that state power, with all its risks and dangers, offers far more stability and freedom than a stateless world. "When states are absent," Snyder declares, "rights—by any definition—are impossible to sustain."[4]

This contrast between Marrus and Snyder calls to mind my discussion in the previous chapter of Carlo Ginzburg and Robert Cover, who offered differing visions of the scholarly mission with consequences for our thinking about history and the historian as witness. In comparing the historian and the witness, Ginzburg emphasized proof as the foundation of the quest for truth—and the antidote to a dangerous historical skepticism that can undermine our epistemological and moral foundations. Cover, while not speaking directly to the role of the witness, nonetheless offered a model of the scholar who can serve as bridge between descriptive and prescriptive tasks, as well as between the real and ideal.

It is easy to regard this set of positions as unbridgeable. But fastidious attention to sources and concern for veracity need not be at odds with the goal of planting the seeds of memory for future generations. Deborah Lipstadt, Richard Evans, Michael Marrus, Timothy Snyder, and Carlo Ginzburg all have a powerful sense of urgency about getting it —that is, history—right; the consequences of their attempts to do so are meaningful not merely to the relatively small cohort of trained historians but to wider audiences possessed of broader concerns than those of the practicing scholar. Ginzburg, after all, sought to use *The Historian and the Judge* to persuade his readership of the legal and moral imperative of freeing his friend from jail. Evans testified at the Lipstadt trial and then wrote about it to ensure that the integrity of history be preserved. Wittingly or not, his testimony and the massive research that undergirded it have served to fortify the collective remembrance of the Shoah.

This is not a new function. Since antiquity, historians have repeatedly moved beyond the simple task of describing to instruct, reproach, and instill memory. In the modern era, when the methodological protocol guiding their work has been defined with greater precision and guarded ever more jealously, historians have used their professional tools to liberate, console, and provide witness, among many other utilities. These aims offer up a portrait of the modern historian that is markedly different from the image of the isolated scholar buried under a mountain of historical data and severed from the vibrant currents of life.

Even with the rising mound of scholarship produced in our day, this cloistered image does not do justice to the historian. I have explored in this book a range of historians who were committed to the proposition that history could and must serve life. At times, they operated in extremis when the stakes of history were most clear to them. History was alternately a lifeline of support, an essential reminder of a monumental past, necessary evidence in a judicial proceeding, or a bridge to the memory of future generations.

It is this last function that brings us back to Yosef Yerushalmi, whose presence has hovered over this book. Much of what has animated me to write it is the desire to reconsider the relationship between history and memory that he proposed in *Zakhor*. I imagine this reconsideration not as a refutation but rather as an intense engagement with and, at the end of the day, an homage to his work. It was Yerushalmi who decisively put in front of us the question of what utility were Jewish history and the historian. It was he who declared that "modern Jewish historiography can never substitute for Jewish memory," that the path of the modern historian had diverged sharply from that of the premodern framer of myth and meaning.[5] But it was also he who proclaimed in *Zakhor* that "the burden of building a bridge to his people remains with the historian."[6] He gestured there and earlier to the notion of the historian as a "physician of memory." This figure seems an apt fit for many of those surveyed in this book, who frequently traversed the border between history and memory.

But is this a good or appropriate function for the modern historian? After all, when assuming such a task, historians must recognize that the possibility of distortion or misrepresentation, intended or not, is always alive, all the more so in trying conditions. Such conditions, it would seem, have inclined Jewish historians to privilege the woes and travails to which Jews were subjected over a more balanced assessment of a stable daily existence marked by periodic persecution. Indeed, when we think of the tradition of "cherishing woes," and when we take stock of all the attention that historians and others have paid to the recollection and commemoration of past tragedies, we must ask, Have the pathways of Jewish memory been irreversibly paved by trauma? Is there an excess of trauma-induced memory?[7]

These questions call to mind the admonition of the Israeli historian and philosopher of science Yehuda Elkana. In a bracing op-ed from 1988, Elkana, who survived Auschwitz as a young child, insisted to his fellow Israelis that "we must learn to *forget!* Today I see no more important political and educational task for the leaders of this nation than to take their stand on the side of life, to dedicate themselves to creating our future, and not to be preoccupied from morning to night with symbols, ceremonies, and lessons of the Holocaust. They must uproot the domination of that historical 'remember!' [zakhor] over our lives."[8]

Elkana's concerns have since been echoed by various observers concerned about the consequences of an excess of memory on contemporary Israeli and Jewish political attitudes and behavior.[9] Among them, the historians Saul Friedlander, Tom Segev, Idith Zertal, and Moshe Zuckermann have questioned whether the regular and ritualized invocation of past tragedies impairs Israeli government policy. They are mindful of the fact that Israeli leaders across the ideological spectrum such as David Ben-Gurion, Abba Eban, Menachem Begin, and Benjamin Netanyahu have frequently invoked the specter of the Holocaust—and the peril of new Hitlers—in articulating policy positions.[10] From a different perspective and in a different context, the American sociologist Arlene Stein has asked whether there is "too much memory" in a chapter of her *Reluctant Witnesses* devoted to the link between Holocaust memory and support for Zionism in America. She has criticized the ease with which the Holocaust has been invoked by advocates on both sides of the Israeli-Palestinian conflict.[11] More generally, questions are arising in Europe and North America about whether the culture of memorializing and teaching about the Holocaust has reached a tipping point: Germans, in particular, wonder whether younger generations born well after the Second World

War can or should face frequent exposure to the history of the Holocaust, whereas in the United States young people have begun to ask whether educational priorities should be placed elsewhere.[12]

These are not new questions, but they are exceptionally important and delicate ones. Punctuated by Yehuda Elkana's cri de coeur, they recall Nietzsche's memorable statement that "without forgetting it is quite impossible to live at all."[13] It is interesting to ask whether forgetting is a necessary precondition to living—or, in reasonable doses, the antidote to an excess of trauma-induced memory.

History as a Tool of Reconciliation

One place to peer into this possibility is in conflict-ridden regions in which competing groups hold to deeply entrenched and opposing historical narratives. Here, in the throes of intense hostility, one can grasp the need to strike a sage balance between remembering and forgetting. If historians in such settings serve only to affirm the historical virtue of their respective groups, then their task as agents of reconciliation would be deeply compromised. In such a context, the path of forgetting—or perhaps disrupting and undoing—the narrative of self-virtue would be the wiser route.

An instructive case is present-day Northern Ireland, still emerging out of the Troubles that afflicted the country from the late 1960s until the Good Friday Agreement of 1998. Essential to the long-term success of the agreement will be the ability of Protestant Unionists and Catholic Republicans to overcome centuries of demonization of each other. Can historians play a productive role, perhaps by disrupting entrenched narratives that divide the world into good and evil? This is the hope of Belfast-based Richard England, who believes that a mix of balance, context, understanding, and openness to counterfactuals enables a "responsible form of public history" that can change perceptions. Another Northern Ireland–based scholar, Cillian McGrattan, maintains that since historical narratives have played a large role in stoking ethnic tensions, historians can and must play a role in challenging, deconstructing, and providing alternatives to one-sided versions. This work may cause tension with public officials who either favor their own group's account of the past or ignore the past altogether. But McGrattan insists that "by bringing a critical voice to the public debate concerning the causes and consequences of past actions, historians have a vital role to play in deepening democracy and justice in post-conflict societies."[14]

In this instance, the historian acts as a surgeon of memory, disassembling whole narrative blocs to disrupt the flow of unhealthy memory, while opening new and healthier passages of historical understanding. Along with this role of dissecting, historians might be able to perform other functions of value, especially in areas riven by conflict.

This is the underlying rationale of the Institute for Historical Justice and Rehabilitation (IHJR) in Leiden. Established in 2004, the Institute has outlined a multistep "theory of change" for conflict zones in which history assumes a central role. The first step calls for historians from "antagonistic communities [to] come together to discuss and construct a shared historical narrative" with the aim of inducing sensitivity to the experience of the other group. Subsequent steps call for scholars to refine and expand the shared narrative, at which point local civil society activists on the ground can begin to disseminate it. The concluding stages call for government bodies to "translate IHJR's work into policies"—in particular, by promoting and implementing acts of reconciliation between antagonistic communities.[15]

The guiding principle of the Institute—that history matters deeply, especially in challenging distorted historical accounts of the "other"—has been applied to a number of global hotspots. The Institute invested time and effort in assembling scholars in the former Yugoslavia, as well as in two of the most intractable cases of political and historical polarization: Armenia/Turkey and Israel/Palestine. In light of the deep chasm dividing these groups on the question of genocide, the Institute convened Armenian and Turkish historians to study the shared historical experiences of their respective groups *prior* to the events of 1915–1923. An abiding aim of this work was to encourage a new measure of openness and sensitivity toward one another—in ways that might prepare the ground for Turks to overcome a century of denial of the mass murder of over one million Armenians and thereby allow their descendants a measure of historical justice by validating their collective memory.[16]

In the case of Israel and Palestine, the Institute brought historians together to explore the starkly divergent experiences of the year 1948: for Jews, it was a year not only of *independence* but of *liberation* from millennia of exile, whereas for Arabs, the year witnessed the mass dispossession of native inhabitants in what came to be known as the Nakba, or "Catastrophe." Rather than seek to produce a seamless shared history, the Institute commissioned a pair of historians, Motti Golani and Adel Manna, a Jewish Israeli and a Palestinian of Israeli citizenship, to produce narratives that were juxtaposed under the title "Two Sides of the Coin: Independence and Nakba, 1948." The authors maintained the hope that exposure to the competing narratives might alter each side's perception of the other, though they could not predict whether that work would precede or follow a more formal process of peace negotiations.[17]

Work of this kind seeks to serve a number of purposes including inculcating greater sensitivity to the other and offering the prospect of healing deep psychic traumas through historical recognition. Both are extremely important in the context of the tortured relations between Jews and Arabs in historic Palestine. Each group's historical memory highlights its own heroism and often the other group's infamy. Throughout much of their shared existence, educators within the two groups fashioned historical curricula that variously ignored or vilified the other. The stakes were and are high, for the longer children are nourished on myths of the heroism of their side and villainy of the other, the more difficult it will be to uproot mutual suspicion. The Oslo peace process, formally inaugurated by Israeli prime minister Yitzhak Rabin and Palestine Liberation Organization (PLO) chairman Yasir Arafat in 1993, lurched forward and back again as it sought to achieve reconciliation between Israelis and Palestinians. Along the way, it set in motion a number of projects focused on altering school curricula and historical perceptions of the other. The loss of momentum in negotiations by the turn of the twenty-first century meant that far-reaching reforms never took hold. Since that time, a nongovernmental effort initiated in 1998 by the Palestinian scholar Sami Adwan and the late Israeli scholar Dan Bar-On under the rubric PRIME (Peace Research Institute in the Middle East) has produced a model textbook of side-by-side historical narratives, "Learning Each Other's Historical Narrative: Palestinians and Israelis."[18] The ongoing work of PRIME is intended for use by teachers in Jewish and Arab schools in Israel and Palestine.

Can historians make a difference in a situation such as this in which there is a total political impasse? After all, they are hardly magicians and rarely master statesmen. But they can be framers of memory and perhaps, in a sense, even group therapists, recovering long-suppressed memories and dissecting unhealthy ones. It is especially helpful if they remember, as Viet Thanh Nguyen powerfully counsels in his recent book exploring competing Vietnamese and American memories of the Vietnam War, that there is much to be gained by remembering not only one's own past but that of others as well.[19] Work of this sort can contribute to paving a path of mutual understanding and reconciliation, though certainly not in isolation from concurrent political and social factors.

In highlighting the Israel-Palestine conflict, I must add a confessional note at this late stage. I approach the ongoing conflict between Jews and Arabs in the land between the Jordan River and Mediterranean Sea not simply as a historian, and surely not as a dispassionate one. I do so as a believing, practicing, politically progressive Jew with a deep and abiding connection to his people *and* a sense of moral urgency in advancing the goal of Palestinian self-determination. These combined commitments prompt me to ask what I (and other historians) can do to bring a measure of peace and justice to both groups in the fraught land they occupy. At least as far as I see it, such an ambition does not deviate from, but rather emerges out of, the lineage of Jewish historical writing that I have attempted to trace in this book.

In recognizing that link, I am not seeking to make a case for the exceptional nature of Jewish history nor of the Israeli-Palestinian conflict as a site of attempted historical reconciliation. Nor, for that matter, do I feel the need to apologize for my own identitarian investment in the object of research. It seems naive and potentially unproductive to believe that we bring a completely blank canvas to the depiction of the past, as I shall suggest in the brief methodological postscript.[20] There is always a fair bit of the background filled in before we engage our sources, owing to environmental, temperamental, and ideological factors. Acknowledging and even embracing the desire to use the past to ameliorate the future—as is the case for me in the Israeli-Palestinian conflict—may guide the way we frame our sources, but it does not mean a descent into anarchic relativism. It does not require the historian to suspend the judicious sifting of evidence. Nor does it diminish the constant imperative to gauge, weigh, and check one's passions. The historian must continue to heed the norms, standards, and protocols of the profession even when propelled by a presentist urge or engaged in a self-consciously constructive act. But that adherence need not and, for better or worse, cannot lead to an evacuation of self or of the guiding impulses that frame our own questions.

And so I am drawn to the self-conscious deployment of history in the Israeli-Palestinian conflict. I am more committed than ever to teaching the histories of Zionist and Palestinian nationalism together, noting the points at which they intersect and those at which they diverge, with a mix of critical distance and empathy. And I am committed to thinking of ways in which history can effect greater understanding and even reconciliation, without forgetting that few may be prepared to listen. Rarely is there a deafening clamor for the historian's labors. And yet, we do possess a valuable asset—rich historical perspective—that can be brought to bear in productive ways. In conditions of political stalemate, the historian can play the role of archaeologist, rummaging through the past in search of that which was discarded by past societies.

If, for example, as many believe, the existing paradigm of diplomatic resolution in the Palestinian-Israeli conflict—the model of a two state solution—has run into a dead end, historians are well positioned to explore the trove of past ideas to determine if something might be of relevance or value.[21] They will discover various versions of the idea of a single state between the Jordan and the Mediterranean. In today's world, Palestinian activists (from Edward Said to Omar Barghouti), Western academics (from Tony Judt to Judith Butler), and Zionist figures (from Israeli settlers to Israeli president Reuven Rivlin) have all espoused versions of a single state, although they have very different understandings of what it would look like. In his book *One State, Two States,* the historian Benny Morris has reviewed earlier plans for a single state, ranging from the Revisionist Zionist Vladimir Jabotinsky's call for a Jewish state on both banks of the Jordan River to the peace-oriented Brit Shalom's proposal for a binational division of power between Jews and Arabs.[22] Morris has also recalled other proposals including a series of confederated arrangements, a canton system that would divide the land according to population concentrations, and various two-state schemes.[23] (Some have even proposed variations on a three-state solution, either through the creation of two states in the West Bank and Gaza alongside Israel or by returning control of the West Bank to Jordan and the Gaza Strip to Egypt.)[24]

After undertaking a wide-ranging review of the past, Morris found little worthy of revival in the present. Under current conditions, he believes that there is scant hope for either a one-state or a two-state solution, or, indeed, anything in between.[25] This may be so at present, but the historian's work is not done. Historians must continue to see the past as an open archive, brimming with discarded or neglected ideas to be retrieved in order to stimulate thinking about the future.[26] To be sure, the past is not the sole repository of creative or constructive thinking for the future, but it is a neglected source. Historical perspective leavens, expands, and elevates our understanding of the world around us.

History's Utilities

Alongside its *archaeological* function, history is also of value to the present in other meaningful ways. It can serve a vital *ethical* function, as Edith Wyschograd has proposed, by giving name to anonymous and forgotten victims of the past whose descendants' pain would be alleviated by a measure of historical val-idation.[27] This work, a kind of restorative justice, is especially important in post-conflict settings, including those in which a truth and reconciliation process has been established.[28] But it can serve a valuable role as well in instances of long-standing and even dormant historical injustices, especially in which the work of remembering is of *another's* travails or pain. An exam-ple of this "alternate ethics of remembering" is the decision by Georgetown University in 2015 to undertake a detailed investi-gation of the institution's sale in 1838 of 272 slaves from which it profited.[29] The university working group entrusted with ex-amining Georgetown's history based its work on the premise that "reconciliation over a marred history can only build on a history-telling that is frank, transparent, and true." It then de-termined that the sale in question was the largest, though not the only, commercial transaction involving slaves owned by the university. Georgetown's president, John J. DiGioia, accepted the committee's various recommendations, which included a call to issue an apology, create an institute for the study of slav-ery, build a public memorial, and offer preferential admission to descendants of the slaves (though not to offer financial assis-tance to them). These proposals rested on a conscious desire to link historical research into Georgetown's slave-owning past to memory of the past, and then to reconciliation as "the final goal of healing history's wounds."[30]

In addition to this type of work, history can also play an im-portant *advisory* function by pointing out successful and unsuc-cessful actions in the past to present-day policy makers. Richard Neustadt and Ernest May taught a course for several decades at Harvard intended for policy makers that relied on case stud-ies that unpacked and dissected the evolution of key govern-ment decisions. The goal of their reliance on history was not to dictate action, as they wrote in *Thinking in Time: The Uses of*

History for Decision Makers. Rather, they proposed "drawing on history to frame sharper questions and doing so systematically, routinely."[31]

More recently, two Harvard scholars, Graham Allison and Niall Ferguson, paid homage in 2016 to *Thinking in Time* when they advanced the idea of a White House Council of Historians to advise the president of the United States. Animating this idea was their call for "a new and rigorous 'applied history'—an attempt to illuminate current challenges and choices by analyzing precedents and historical analogues."[32] It is this principle that anchors the Applied History Project that Allison and Ferguson co-chair at Harvard.

In a related vein, historians Jo Guldi and David Armitage issued a sweeping "history manifesto" in 2014 with the objective of encouraging historians to think in larger swaths of time in order to capture deep structural patterns in the past. They point to the capacity of Big Data to aggregate massive amounts of information as a boon to identifying these long-term patterns. Their call for a return to "long-termism" is key, in their view, to "renewing the connection between past and future."[33]

Such an approach raises the prospect that a certain kind of historical work can even have a *predictive* utility. Eric Hobsbawm proceeded cautiously toward the conclusion that historians, while manifestly not prophets, can engage in forecasting and prediction, not of particular events, but of larger social trends that come into view through a close reading of the past. "History," Hobsbawm asserted, "cannot get away from the future, if only because there is no line which divides the two."[34]

Whether one subscribes to this predictive potential or not, there is a growing willingness to explore the ways that history can play a more visible role in public debate and policy deliberations oriented toward the future.[35] At the same time, it is important to recall that historians do not necessarily agree with one another about the past—or, for that matter, the future. Deep and often bitter divisions separate scholars of Israel-Palestine, for example, and not only according to predictable national boundaries. Israeli scholars of differing generations (and even those who belong to the same generation) have very different views of the past and how to record it.[36] The same could be said about historians writing anywhere on any subject.

But the absence of consensus should not prevent us from insisting that historical knowledge be an essential ingredient in thinking about and even planning for the future. Historians may be imperfect bearers of such knowledge, but they are the best we have—and often they are pretty good. The figures examined in this book typically used their deep knowledge of the past with an eye toward the future. They would have answered the simple question that opens Marc Bloch's *The Historian's Craft*, and with which I opened this book—"What is the use of history?—in an abundance of ways. But all would have imagined, at least the modern scholars among them, that there were multiple uses for history. Many would have readily traversed the boundary between history and memory, had they been aware of its existence. Most would have sided with Yosef Yerushalmi, who, while acknowledging Nietzsche's romance with forgetting, nevertheless asserted that if forced to choose, he would opt for "the side of 'too much' rather than 'too little'" history.[37]

In that same moment, Yerushalmi pointed to an important constructive role for history when he asserted that the "antonym of 'forgetting' is not 'remembering' but 'justice.'"[38] In this important and ultimate regard, I am in complete agreement with Yerushalmi. For with a sufficient dose of history, one can begin to approach the demands of both memory and justice that are captured in the timeless African proverb, with its powerful Benjaminian echoes: "Until the lion has his or her own storyteller, the hunter will always have the best part of the story."[39] And yet, while helping to rescue the story of the victim, the historian must never cease to acknowledge other voices in a given historical moment, as well as the humanizing mandate to capture their rich diversity.

A Brief Reflection on Method

It is unusual, to be sure, to offer a set of reflections such as these *after* the conclusion to a book, all the more so when they deal with the method putatively used *throughout* the book. Of course, it is almost as unusual—and perhaps a bit self-indulgent—for a historian to take the time to lay out his or her guiding theoretical principles, primitive as they may be.

And yet I take seriously Samuel Moyn's admonition that we all too often outsource this task to professional philosophers of history.[1] As in other fields, this has generally been the case in Jewish history, though there are a number of notable exceptions, such as Salo W. Baron in *The Contemporary Relevance of History* (1986) and Moshe Rosman in *How Jewish Is Jewish History?* (2007).[2] I, for my part, am not a philosopher, nor is this book intended as a full-blown philosophy of history. But it does seem responsible to take up Moyn's challenge to try to articulate how I go about the work of historical interpretation.

From the advent of my formal professional training, I have been drawn to two conflicting sensibilities: a strong belief, nurtured by the riches of the archive, that the historian must seek to reconstruct the past meticulously in the quest to *approach* truth; and, in tension with that belief, a persistent pull toward various forms of constructivist accounts of historical method focused on the recognition that we are unable to do what Ranke aspired to do as a historian: "extinguish myself in order that the things could speak [for themselves]."[3] The tension between these two sensibilities became clear to me upon first encounter with Roland Barthes's 1967 essay "The Discourse of History." It was a jolt to a young graduate student to have to grapple with Barthes's suggestion that "the narration of past events" was not different "in some indubitably distinctive feature, from imaginary narration, as we find it in the epic, the novel, and the drama."[4] Barthes's identification of narrativity as the shared and open border between history and fiction produced in me less a belief in the unavoidable indeterminacy of historical interpretation than a newfound sensitivity to the process of crafting *historia rerum gestarum,* the narration of the events of the past.

One of the most significant elucidators of Barthes's position was Hayden White, whose monumental *Metahistory* expanded our understanding of the nature of modern historical writing by categorizing works according to differing modes of emplotment, argument, and ideology. With respect to the last category, ideology, White argued that nineteenth-century historians were ideological not so much by virtue of their political or polemical stances but to the extent that they came to regard the *form* of the historical narrative as "a content or essence." In doing so, they conflated *historia rerum gestarum,* the narration of the past, and *res gestae,* what actually happened.[5] Roland Barthes and then White flipped this somewhat unwitting conflation on its head by asserting that historical narrative bore strong similarities to and, in fact, assumed the properties of fictional narrative. In doing so, they challenged the underlying logic of a naive historical "realism," as well as its closely related source of methodological validation, objectivity.[6]

I was intrigued and compelled by this kind of sharp, semiotically inspired critique of my emerging craft. Over time, though, I came to realize that it was hard to follow or accept fully their analysis of history as akin, in form, to fiction—in no small part because I clung to a shred (or more) of the realist credo that guides most practicing historians.[7] In forging my own view of the matter, I was stimulated and challenged both by White and by his forceful critic, Carlo Ginzburg, to whom reference was made in Chapter 3. The polemic between them at the 1990 conference *Nazism and the "Final Solution"* and then in the ensuing volume, *Probing the Limits,* carved out a nuanced historiographical space between the poles of an unvarnished realism on one hand and wholesale surrender to the literary, imagined, and fictive qualities of historiography on the other.[8]

In seeking to understand that position more fully, we might profitably turn back to some of the most incisive thinkers about history from the past century. One recalls, for example, the Italian philosopher Benedetto Croce, who insisted, "Where there is no narrative, there is no history."[9] Closely aligned with Croce was the Oxford philosopher and historian R. B. Collingwood, mentioned in the Introduction, who translated Croce and was in correspondence with him. Both men affirmed a simple and intuitive claim: the historian stands at the center of historiographical production. For Croce, this principle was best expressed in his 1912 aphorism "All history is contemporary history." The historian's angle of observation onto the past is shaped by present-day preoccupations that animate and inform his or her work.[10]

Meanwhile, Collingwood understood that "the only possible knowledge of the past is mediate or inferential or indirect, never empirical." His particular reformulation of this commonplace notion, in the posthumously published *The Idea of History* (1946), was the theory of "re-enactment." The historian, Collingwood wrote, must not merely seek to comprehend an earlier text in exact philological terms; rather, he must understand how and why the author of that text chose to solve the key problems in it in the way he did. This places on the historian the obligation of "re-thinking for himself the thought of his author"—or "re-enact[ing] the past in his own mind."[11]

This kind of mental construction, keenly attentive but not

altogether subordinate to the primary source, is a fair description of what the historian does. But an objection can be quickly raised: if we turn to history for empirical validation of the past in order to understand the present better, but recognize that our knowledge is simply a construct of the individual historian's mind, are we not consigned to an incapacitating relativism? Not necessarily, Collingwood responds; with respect to reenactment, we need not assume that "because it is subjective, [it] cannot be objective." After all, someone who engages in "an act of knowing" can both do that and be aware that he or she is performing that act.[12] Moreover, the fact that one reenacts the past does not mean that one invents it out of whole cloth. The quality of one's historical labors relies on the credible use of sources, analytical rigor, and a compelling narrative, all regulated by the consensual norms of the profession. Those criteria cannot guarantee Truth, but they do differentiate between more and less convincing versions of the past—and help propel us to what Collingwood wisely calls "relative truth."[13]

Notes

Unless otherwise identified translations are mine.

Introduction

1. Marc Bloch, *The Historian's Craft,* translated by Peter Putnam (New York: Vintage, 1953), 43. President Obama's reflections on history were delivered at the memorial service for Rev. Pinckney, one of those murdered in a Charleston church by the white supremacist Dylann Roof on 17 June 2015. Obama's remarks, and the Charleston murder, helped stimulate a debate in the South over the wisdom and morality of keeping Confederate symbols (e.g., flags and statues) in places of public prominence. See "Remarks by the President in Eulogy for the Honorable Reverend Clementa Pinckney," White House, Office of the Press Secretary, at https://www.whitehouse.gov/ the-press-office/2015/06/26/remarks-president-eulogy-honorable-reverend -clementa-pinckney.

2. The question is articulated anew with concision by Lynn Hunt in Hunt, *Writing History in the Global Era* (New York: Norton, 2014), 1.

3. See, for example, by Gordon Hutner and Feisel G. Mohamed, "The Real Humanities Crisis Is Happening at Public Universities," New Republic Online, 6 September 2013; and Diana E. Sheets, "The Crisis in the Humanities: Why Today's Educational and Cultural Experts Can't and Won't Resolve the Failings of the Liberal Arts," *Huffington Post,* 5 July 2013 (updated 14 September 2013), http://www.huffingtonpost. com/dr-diana-e-sheets/the-crisis-in-the-humanit_b_3588171.html. The Harvard report noted a 4 percent drop in humanities concentrators at Harvard from 2003 to 2012, and a larger, 16 percent drop (when history was included) over a sixty-year period from 1954: "Addressing a Decline in Humanities Enrollment," *Harvard Magazine,* 5 June 2013.

4. Michael Bérubé, "The Humanities Declining? Not According to the Numbers," *Chronicle of Higher Education,* 1 July 2013, available at http://chronicle.com/article/The-Humanities-Declining-Not/140093/. For a related argument, focused on women's decreasing interest in the

humanities, see Heidi Tworek, "The Real Reason the Humanities Are 'in Crisis,'" *Atlantic*, 18 December 2013.

5. Gerda Lerner, "The Necessity of History," in Lerner, *Why History Matters: Life and Thought* (New York: Oxford University Press, 1997), 115.

6. Ibid., 116.

7. See Blaine Greteman's helpful grounding of the current "crisis" in a broader six-hundred year history in "It's the End of the Humanities as We Know It: And I Feel Fine," *New Republic*, 13 June 2014, available at http:// www.newrepublic.com/article/118139/crisis-humanities-has-long-history.

8. It is this potential that leads Jo Guldi and David Armitage to acknowledge in their *History Manifesto* that history allows us to "look past the parochial concerns of disciplines too attached to client funding, the next business cycle, or the next election" to see the larger picture. The book by Guldi and Armitage has generated a great deal of controversy, particularly their claim that historical research today succumbs to what they call "short-termism," the tendency of scholars to chew off ever smaller chunks of time in their studies. See Jo Guldi and David Armitage, *The History Manifesto* (Cambridge: Cambridge University Press, 2014), 2–3, 7. For a sharp critique that disputes the proposition that historical studies are becoming more short term in scale (and that long-scale studies are particularly valuable for policy debates), see the contribution by Deborah Cohen and Peter Mandler to the *American Historical Review* forum on *The History Manifesto*, "*The History Manifesto:* A Critique," *American Historical Review* 120 (April 2015): 530–542. See also the forum on the *Manifesto* sponsored by the leading French journal *Annales: Histoire, Sciences Sociales* 2 (April–June 2015), in particular Lynn Hunt, "Faut-il réinitialiser l'histoire?" 319–325, and Claudia Moatti, "L'e-story ou le nouveau mythe hollywoodien," 327–332.

9. The eminent women's scholar Joan Scott, for example, has described her task as a historian as "avowedly political: to point out and change inequalities between women and men." Over the course of her career, and especially in *Gender and the Politics of History,* Scott has sought to trace the constantly shifting meaning of categories such as "men" and "women" with an eye toward dissolving the power hierarchies that have repeatedly privileged the former over the latter. See Joan Scott, *Gender and the Politics of History* (New York: Columbia University Press, 1988), 5–7.

10. John Hope Franklin, *Mirror to America: The Autobiography of John Hope Franklin* (New York: Farrar, Straus and Giroux, 2005), 226. On the link between historical knowledge and social change, Franklin once observed: "I think knowing one's history leads one to act in a more enlight-

ened fashion. I can not imagine how knowing one's history would not urge one to be an activist." Franklin's quote from *Emerge* (March 1994) is available at http://jhfc.duke.edu/johnhopefranklin/quotes.html (accessed on 25 January 2015).

11. Patrick J. Geary, *The Myth of Nations* (Princeton: Princeton University Press, 2002), 15. Geary wrote his book in the wake of the collapse of the Soviet Union, which, among other effects, unleashed a torrent of ethnic chauvinism across the newly reconfigured European continent. He called to task historians, even "reputable scholars (who) are drawn in to the polemical uses of the past," by reifying and then mythologizing fluid concepts such as the nation (8).

12. Margaret MacMillan, *Dangerous Games: The Uses and Abuses of History* (New York: Modern Library, 2008), 72, 84 (quotation).

13. My own preoccupation with the problematic of historicism commenced with the first scholarly article that I published: "The Scholem-Kurzweil Debate and Modern Jewish Historiography," *Modern Judaism* 6 (1986): 261–286. It dealt with the critique during the 1960s by the Israeli literary scholar Baruch Kurzweil of the historicization of Judaism by modern scholars, especially by Kurzweil's main nemesis, Gershom Scholem. Of particular note was Kurzweil's Nietzschean-inspired "On the Use and Abuse of Jewish Studies," in which Kurzweil praised the great German philosopher, who "understood well the danger of historicism. . . . More than history reveals, it all too frequently covers up." See Kurzweil, "'Al ha-to'let veha-nezek shebe-mada'e ha-Yahadut," in his *Be-ma'avak 'al 'erkhe ha-Yahadut* (Jerusalem: Schocken, 1969), 221.

14. Friedrich Nietzsche, *On the Advantage and Disadvantage of History for Life,* translated by Peter Preuss (Indianapolis: Hackett, 1980), 11.

15. Nietzsche, *On the Advantage and Disadvantage of History for Life,* 14.

16. On the perils of objectivity in Nietzsche's thinking about history, see Mark Sinclair, "Nietzsche and the Problem of History," *Richmond Journal of Philosophy* 8 (Winter 2004): 1–6. Nietzsche's essay, which, we recall, focused on the use *and* abuse of history, had more tempered moments alongside its withering critique. Thus, he affirmed with equanimity that "the unhistorical and the historical are equally necessary for the health of an individual, a people, and a culture." Nietzsche, *On the Advantage and Disadvantage of History for Life,* 10.

17. Yosef Hayim Yerushalmi, *Zakhor: Jewish History and Jewish Memory,* rev. ed. (New York: Schocken, 1989), 86, 94, 101. Yerushalmi invoked Nietzsche in an epilogue to a revised edition of *Zakhor.* Titled "Postscript: Reflections on Forgetting," it was based on a talk he gave in France in

June 1987. See *Zakhor*, 106–107. Yehuda Kurtzer attempts a constructive reframing of memory in relationship to history in *Shuva: The Future of the Jewish Past* (Waltham, Mass.: Brandeis University Press, 2012), as well as David G. Roskies' literary treatment of Jewish sites of memory, *The Jewish Search for a Usable Past* (Bloomington: Indiana University Press, 1999). Meanwhile, for a lucid discussion of the history of Jewish historiography, see Michael Brenner, *Prophets of the Past: Interpreters of Jewish History*, translated by Steven Rendall (Princeton: Princeton University Press, 2010). At various points in this chapter, Brenner's and my interests and narrative trajectories overlap, as, for instance, in our common discussion of Jacques Basnage and Hannah Adams, as well as of Zeev Yawetz and Berel Wein. This may be due to the fact that Brenner is not only a friend and colleague but also a student of the same teacher, Yosef Yerushalmi. In any event, I am indebted to Brenner and his work, even as I seek to define a distinctive set of guiding motifs for modern Jewish historiography. For more on modern Jewish historiography, see the important collection by Ismar Schorsch, *From Text to Context: The Turn to History in Modern Judaism* (Hanover, N.H.: Brandeis University Press, 1994), as well as Lionel Kochan, *The Jew and His History* (London: Macmillan, 1977), and Reuven Michael, *Ha-ketivah ha-historit ha-Yehudit: meha-Renesans 'ad ha-'et ha-ḥadashah* (Jerusalem: Mosad Bialik, 1993).

18. Yerushalmi, *Zakhor*, 8.

19. Ibid., 16. Nietzsche, for his part, offered a far less charitable set of images, comparing modern humans unfavorably to a herd of grazing animals whose contentment lay in their ability to forget all and live in the moment. Unlike the forgetful cow, we are addled by a "surfeit of history" that stands as an obstacle—indeed, is "hostile and dangerous"—to life. Nietzsche, *On the Advantage and Disadvantage of History for Life*, 8, 28. Nietzsche suggested that in his day "a race of eunuchs" presided over the fetishistic cult of history in its modern guise (29, 31).

20. Yerushalmi, *Zakhor*, 102.

21. Among the scholarly luminaries who responded to or wrote about the book in the years after its appearance were Harold Bloom, Robert Bonfil, Robert Chazan, Amos Funkenstein, and Michael A. Meyer. On the twenty-fifth anniversary of *Zakhor*'s appearance, the *Jewish Quarterly Review* hosted a symposium to assess the book's impact that included Moshe Idel, Peter Miller, Gavriel Rosenfeld, Sidra DeKoen Ezrahi, and Amnon Raz-Krakotzkin. See *Jewish Quarterly Review* 97 (2007): 291–543.

22. William H. McNeill has made the point sharply, perhaps overly so, in his 1985 essay "Why Study History?" There McNeill asserts: "Historical

knowledge is no more and no less than carefully and critically constructed collective memory. As such it can both make us wiser in our public choices and more richly human in our private lives." McNeill, "Why Study History?" at American Historical Association website, http://www .historians.org/about-aha-and-membership/aha-history-and-archives/ archives/why-study-history-%281985%29 (accessed on 23 December 2014).

23. Wilhelm Dilthey, *Der Aufbau der geschictlichen Welt in den Geisteswissenschaften* (Stuttgart: Teubner, 1973), 261, quoted in Jeffrey Andrew Barash, "Collective Memory and Historical Time," *Práticas da História* 1 (2016): 16. Barash offers a helpful and searching examination of the idea of "collective memory," noting that it is "marked by discontinuity and flux brought on by the arrival of new generations and gradual demise of older contemporaries" (28). Aleida Assmann provides a periodization of the relationship between history and memory, concluding (and identifying) with the current phase of "interactions between memory and history" in which the historian can and does play a productive role: Aleida Assmann, "Transformations Between History and Memory," *Social Research: An Interdisciplinary Quarterly* 75 (2008): 61. See also Jan Assmann, "Collective Memory and Cultural Identity," *New German Critique* 65 (1995): 125–133, and the comprehensive survey in Geoffrey Cubitt, *History and Memory* (Manchester: Manchester University Press, 2007).

24. Pierre Nora, *Les Lieux de mémoire: La République* (Paris: Gallimard, 1984), xix, translated by Arthur Goldhammer as *Realms of Memory: The Construction of the French Past* (New York: Columbia University Press, 1996), 3. The initial exchange with Yerushalmi took place at a conference at Schloss Elmau, Germany, in the summer of 2000; revised versions of the presentations were published in Michael Brenner and David N. Myers, eds. *Jüdische Geschichtsschreibung heute: Themen, Positionen, Kontroversen.* (Munich: Beck Verlag, 2002). See in that volume David N. Myers, "Selbstreflexion in modernen Errinerungsdiskurs," 55–74, and Yosef Hayim Yerushalmi, "Jüdische Historiographie und Postmodernismus: Eine abweichende Meinung," 75–94 (quotations at 76–77).

25. Yerushalmi, "Jüdische Historiographie und Postmodernismus," 75.

26. In overt fashion, this theme anchors my essay "History and Memory in Jewish Studies: Overcoming the Chasm," in Mitchell B. Hart and Tony Michels, eds., *The Cambridge History of Judaism,* vol. 8: *The Modern World, 1815–2000* (Cambridge: Cambridge University Press, 2017), 804–830. My first book, based on the Columbia University dissertation I wrote under Yerushalmi's direction, attempts to excavate the wide space between critical history and collective memory. See *Re-Inventing the*

Jewish Past: European Jewish Intellectuals and the Zionist Return to History (New York: Oxford University Press, 1995).

27. Amos Funkenstein, "Collective Memory and Historical Consciousness," *History and Memory* 1 (Spring–Summer 1989): 21. See also David N. Myers, "Remembering *Zakhor:* A Super-Commentary," *History and Memory* 4 (1992): 129–146.

28. Two prominent Jewish historians arrived at a similar conclusion twenty years ago. In a forum sponsored by the Association for Jewish Studies on *Zakhor* in 1986, Robert Chazan argued that one can read between the lines of Yerushalmi's words to see "an alternative kind of healing function for the Jewish historian." Michael A. Meyer declared that "historians, like midrashists, are interpreters that fasten upon significant passages in their sources and seek to spin out of them a larger story." See "Responses to Yerushalmi's *Zakhor,*" *AJS Newsletter* 36 (Fall 1986): 12, 14.

29. Yosef Hayim Yerushalmi, *Freud's Moses: Judaism Terminable and Interminable* (New Haven: Yale University Press, 1991), 81–100.

30. Yosef Hayim Yerushalmi "A Jewish Historian in the 'Age of Aquarius,'" Commencement Address, Hebrew College, Brookline, Massachusetts, June 1970, reprinted in David N. Myers and Alexander Kaye, eds. *The Faith of Fallen Jews: Yosef Hayim Yerushalmi and the Writing of Jewish History* (Hanover, N.H.: Brandeis University Press, 2014), 52–53.

31. Yerushalmi "A Jewish Historian in the 'Age of Aquarius,'" 57, 58–59. See Eugen Rosenstock-Huessy, *Out of Revolution: Autobiography of Western Man* (New York: Morrow, 1964), 696.

32. Yerushalmi, *Freud's Moses,* 2.

33. Ibid., 30–33, 78.

34. Ibid., 86.

35. Yerushalmi's masterful first book, based on his Columbia University dissertation, was devoted to the life and journeys of a Spanish *converso* who left the Iberian Peninsula to live an open Jewish life in Italy. See Yosef Hayim Yerushalmi, *From Spanish Court to Italian Ghetto: Isaac Cardoso, A Study in Seventeenth-Century Marranism and Jewish Apologetics* (New York: Columbia University Press, 1971). He remained keenly interested in the subject throughout his career.

36. Yerushalmi, "Sur Baer et *Galout,*" in Y. F. Baer, *Galout: L'imaginaire de l'exil dans le judaïsme,* translated into French by Marc de Launay (Paris: Calman-Lévy, 2000), 27, 40, 47. See also the German original: Jizchak Baer, *Galut* (Berlin: Schocken, 1936). I extend thanks to my former student and conversation partner Moshe Lapin, for insisting that this text of Yerushalmi's required closer scrutiny.

37. Yerushalmi, "Sur Baer et *Galout*," 42.

38. Yerushalmi, "Sur Baer et *Galout*," 19–21, and 26.

39. Peter Gay and Gerald J. Cavanaugh, eds., *Historians at Work*, vol. 1: *Herodotus to Froissart* (New York: Harper and Row, 1972), xx. It is important to recall, as the historian Ethan Kleinberg reminded me in a personal communication, that Herodotus was also known as "the father of lies," due to the imaginative tales he inserted into his historical accounts.

40. Friedlander's mediating position, drawn in part from Funkenstein's category of historical consciousness, is clearly spelled out in Friedlander, *Memory, History, and the Extermination of the Jews of Europe* (Bloomington: Indiana University Press, 1993), viii. I should note that my first exposure to major questions of historical interpretation came in Friedlander's seminar at Tel Aviv University in 1983. A bit less than a decade later, I joined him as a colleague in the UCLA History Department.

41. This notion bears resemblance to the Greek grammatical notion of the "middle voice," of which Hayden White (about whom more presently) has made notable and controversial use in theorizing about the writing of history. See White, "Writing in the Middle Voice," *Stanford Literary Review* 9 (1992): 179–187, and his contribution, "Historical Emplotment and the Problem of Truth," in Saul Friedlander, ed., *Probing the Limits of Representation: Nazism and the "Final Solution"* (Cambridge: Harvard University Press, 1992), 37–53. For a related site of mediation, see Jan Assman's notion of mnemohistory, which is "concerned not with the past as such, but only with the past as it is remembered," in Assmann, *Moses the Egyptian: The Memory of Egypt in Western Monotheism* (Cambridge: Harvard University Press, 1997), 9.

42. One indication of the duration of this debate might be that the journal *History and Memory* has continued to be published since 1989. Its first issue hardly marked the birth of the debate, but rather was the realization of an emerging body of mature research on the relationship.

43. Halbwach's canonical *La Mémoire collective* from 1950 has been translated as *On Collective Memory*, edited, translated, and with an introduction by Lewis Coser (Chicago: University of Chicago Press, 1992). See Yerushalmi, *Zakhor*, xxxv. See also Alon Confino, "Collective Memory and Cultural History: Problems of Method," *American Historical Review* 102, no. 5 (December 1997): 1386–1403.

44. R. G. Collingwood, *The Idea of History*, edited by Jan Van Der Dussen (Oxford: Oxford University Press, 1993), 282–283.

45. A recent survey of the North American–based Association for Jewish Studies membership undertaken by the sociologist Steven Cohen

revealed that 85 percent of the field identified as Jewish and 15 percent
as Christian (5 percent), Muslim (1 percent), other (1 percent), or none
(8 percent). Of those who identified as Jewish, 25 percent described
themselves as "just Jewish," that is, without denominational affiliation.
See Steven M. Cohen, "Profiling the Jewish Studies Profession in North
America Highlights from the Survey of AJS Members," 15 July 2015, at
http://www.ajsnet.org/surveys/AJS-2014-Full-Survey-Report.pdf.

46. Initially, some of the first professors at the Freie Universität in Berlin, where the first postwar program was established in 1963, were Jews:
Jacob Taubes, Adolf Leschnitzer, and Michael Landmann. Over time, as
the number of programs expanded, non-Jews came to dominate the field.
Christoph Schulte discusses the transition from an earlier philologically
inclined *Judaistik* to a more methodologically diverse Jewish studies in
"Judaistik or Jewish Studies? The New Construction of Jewish Studies
at the University of the Former German Democratic Republic," *Shofar*
15 (1997): 32–40. For a sharp counterargument, see Peter Schäfer, "Jewish
Studies in Germany Today," *Jewish Studies Quarterly* 3 (1996): 146–161.

47. On the *Historikerstreit,* see Peter Baldwin, *Hitler, the Holocaust and
the Historians Dispute* (Boston: Beacon, 1990), and Richard J. Evans, *In
Hitler's Shadow: West German Historians and the Attempt to Escape the
Nazi Past* (New York: Pantheon, 1989).

48. See Tobias Brinkman, "Memory and Modern Jewish History in
Contemporary Germany," *Shofar* 4 (1997): 17–18.

49. Birgit Klein assembled some data on the composition and motives
of Jewish studies students in Germany, most of whom were non-Jewish,
in "Warum studieren in Deutschland Nichtjüdinnen und Nichtjuden
Judaistik?" *Judaica* 49 (March 1993): 33–41.

50. For a recent critique of "identity politics," see Mark Lilla, "The
End of Identity Liberalism," *New York Times,* 18 November 2017. To be
sure, "identity politics" as an imbalanced, unreflexive, and one-dimensional
apologia for the claims of a given group has little merit. But it is a
different matter when identity politics seeks to "assert or reclaim ways of
understanding their distinctiveness that challenge dominant oppressive
characterizations": Cressida Heyes, "Identity Politics," *Stanford Encyclope-
dia of Philosophy,* 16 July 2002, at http://plato.stanford.edu/entries/identity
-politics (accessed on 16 January 2016). See also James Clifford, "Taking
Identity Politics Seriously: The Contradictory, Stony Ground . . . " in Paul
Gilroy, Lawrence Grossberg, and Angela McRobbie, eds. *Without Guar-
antees: Essays in Honour of Stuart Hall* (London: Verso, 2000), 94–112.

Chapter 1
History as Liberation

1. Later in the century, Wilhelm Dilthey emphasized the importance of imaginative acts of re-creation as an essential step toward a liberating *Verstehen* (or understanding). Dilthey did not believe that one could or should "extinguish oneself," as Ranke did. In anticipation of Collingwood, he wrote that "the highest form of understanding in which the totality of mental life is active [is] re-creating or re-living." Through this mental work of imaginative empathy, one can achieve Verstehen: "Man, tied and limited by the reality of life is liberated not only by art . . . but also by historical understanding." See "Empathy, Re-creating and Re-living" in Wilhelm Dilthey, *Selected Writings,* edited by H. P. Rickman (Cambridge: Cambridge University Press, 1976), 226, 228. See also the account by the important Dilthey scholar Rudolf A. Makkreel, *Dilthey: Philosopher of the Human Studies* (Princeton: Princeton University Press, 1975), 54.

2. Arthur Schlesinger, Jr., "The Causes of the American Civil War: A Note on Historical Sentimentalism," *Partisan Review* 16 (October 1949), 981. Butterfield flatly asserted: "It is part and parcel of the whig interpretation of history that it studies the past with reference to the present." *The Whig Interpretation of History* (London: G. Bell, 1931), 11.

3. Butterfield recants in *The Englishman and His History:* "We are all of us exultant and unrepentant whigs." Herbert Butterfield, *The Englishman and His History* (Hamden, Conn.: Archon, 1970), 3.

4. Walzer introduces his book by stating that it is "about an idea of great presence and power in Western political thought, the idea of a deliverance from suffering and oppression: this-worldly redemption, liberation, redemption." Michael Walzer, *Exodus and Revolution* (New York: Basic, 1985), ix.

5. See Gerda Lerner, *Living with History/Making Social Change* (Chapel Hill: University of North Carolina Press, 2009); Howard Zinn, *You Can't Be Neutral on a Moving Train: A Personal History of Our Times* (Boston: Beacon, 1994).

6. Many historians aim only to get the past right. Lerner and Zinn had a different "regime of historicity," to borrow François Hartog's term. They understood their work as focused on effecting change for the future (and thus belong to the pre-presentist era in Hartog's taxonomy). See Hartog, *Régimes d'historicité: présentisme et expérience du temps* (Paris: Éditions du Seuil, 2003).

7. Howard Zinn, "The Uses of Scholarship," in *Howard Zinn on History* (New York: Seven Stories, 2001), 187.

8. Basnage mixed chronological and thematic approaches in his multiple volumes, saving a running account of Jewish history from the eighth to the eighteenth century for the last volume. See Jacques Basnage, *The History of the Jews, from Jesus Christ to the Present Time: Containing Their Antiquities, Their Religion, Their Rites, the Dispersion of the Ten Tribes in the East and the Persecutions This Nation Has Suffer'd in the West. Being a Supplement and Continuation of the History of Josephus*, translated by Tho. Taylor (London: J. Beaver and B. Lintot, 1708), 1: vi–x. See also Yosef Hayim Yerushalmi, *Zakhor: Jewish History and Jewish Memory* (Seattle: University of Washington Press, 1982), 81–82, and Michael Brenner, *Prophets of the Past: Interpreters of Jewish History*, translated by Steven Rendall (Princeton: Princeton University Press, 2010), 18–19.

9. Basnage, *The History of the Jews*, 1: 2.

10. Ibid., 1: 1.

11. Ibid., 1: 2–3. See also Brenner, *Prophets of the Past*, 19, and Jonathan M. Elukin, "Jacques Basnage and the History of the Jews: Anti-Catholic Polemic and Historical Allegory in the Republic of Letters," *Journal of the History of Ideas* 53, no. 4 (October–December 1992): 603–630.

12. Hannah Adams, *History of the Jews from the Destruction of Jerusalem to the Present Time*, 2 vols. (Boston: J. Eliot, Jr., 1812), 2: 325–326.

13. Ibid., 2: 330–331.

14. Ibid., 1: vi. See Brenner, *Prophets of the Past*, 20.

15. Leopold Zunz, "Etwas über die rabbinische Litteratur," *Maurer'schen Buchandlung* (1818), reprinted in Zunz, *Gesammelte Schriften* (Berlin: Verlag Louis Lamm, 1919), 1: 5.

16. Zunz, "On Rabbinic Literature," in Paul Mendes-Flohr and Jehuda Reinharz, eds., *The Jew in the Modern World: A Documentary History* (New York: Oxford University Press, 2011), 247, 250 ("Etwas," 1: 4, 24). But for a view of Zunz that questions the central role of history and historical thinking in his work, see Amos Bitzan, "Leopold Zunz and the Meanings of *Wissenschaft*," *Journal of the History of Ideas* 78 (April 2017): 233–254.

17. See Charles R. Bambach, *Heidegger, Dilthey, and the Crisis of Historicism* (Ithaca: Cornell University Press, 1995), Thomas A. Howard, *Religion and the Rise of Historicism: W. M. L. de Wette, Jacob Burckhardt and the Theological Origins of Nineteenth-Century Historical Consciousness* (Cambridge: Cambridge University Press, 2000), and David N. Myers, *Resisting History: Historicism and Its Discontents in German-Jewish Thought* (Princeton: Princeton University Press, 2003). For a challenge to the view that a "crisis of historicism" afflicted European intellectual culture in the late nineteenth and early twentieth centuries, see Frederick Beiser, *The*

German Historicist Tradition (Oxford and New York: Oxford University Press, 2011), 24ff.

18. Leopold Zunz, "Die jüdische Literatur" (1845) in Zunz, *Gesammelte Schriften*, 1: 59. See also Michael A. Meyer, Michael Brenner, and Mordechai Breuer, *German-Jewish History in Modern Times: Emancipation and Acculturation* (New York: Columbia University Press, 1997), 135. On Zunz and Wissenschaft more generally, see the standard works of Michael A. Meyer, *The Origins of the Modern Jew* (Detroit: Wayne State University Press, 1967), and Ismar Schorsch, *From Text to Context: The Turn to History in Modern Judaism* (Hanover, N.H.: Brandeis University Press, 1994). Schorsch has recently written a biography of Zunz based on an exhaustive survey of available archival sources: *Leopold Zunz: Creativity in Adversity* (Philadelphia: University of Pennsylvania Press, 2016).

19. The most comprehensive study of Beer's life and thought is Louise Hecht, *Ein jüdischer Aufklärer in Böhmen: Der Pädagoge und Reformer Peter Beer (1758–1838)* (Cologne: Böhlau, 2008). See also Michael Brenner, "Between Haskalah and Kabbalah: Peter Beer's History of Jewish Sects," in Elisheva Carlebach, John M. Efron, and David N. Myers, eds., *Jewish History and Jewish Memory: Essays in Honor of Yosef Hayim Yerushalmi* (Hanover, N.H.: Brandeis University Press, 1998), 389–404, as well as David N. Myers, "Peter Beer in Prague: Probing the Boundaries of Modern Jewish Historiography," in H. Amstutz et al., eds., *Fuzzy Boundaries: Festschrift für Antonio Loprieno* (Hamburg: Widmaier Verlag, 2015), 705–714.

20. Peter Beer, *Geschichte, Lehren und Meinungen aller bestandenen und noch bestehenden religiösen Sekten der Juden und der Geheimlehre oder Kabbalah*, 2 vols. (Brünn: J. G. Trassler, 1822, 1823), 2: x–xii.

21. Yosef Kaplan, "'Karaites' in Early Eighteenth-Century Amsterdam," in David S. Katz and Jonathan Israel, eds. *Sceptics, Millenarians, and Jews* (Leiden: Brill, 1990), 203–204. Kaplan notes da Costa's two references to Karaites, though he also notes that da Costa does not identify with the movement. On Beer, see Michael A. Meyer, *Response to Modernity: A History of the Reform Movement in Judaism* (New York: Oxford University Press, 1988), 153.

22. Kaplan, "'Karaites' in Early Eighteenth-Century Amsterdam," 228–229.

23. In recent decades, Amnon Raz-Krakotzkin has insisted with singular force and insight that Protestant theology, especially regarding exile, left a deep imprint on modern Jewish collective—and particularly, Zionist—identities. See Raz-Krakotzkin's iconic article, "Galut mi-tokh

ribonut: 'shelilat ha-galut be-tarbut ha-Yisre'elit," *Te'oryah u-vikoret* 4 (1993): 23–55, and 5 (1994): 113–135, as well as his "Zionist Return to the West and the Mizrachi Jewish Perspective," in Ivan Kalmar and Derek Penslar, eds., *Orientalism and the Jews* (Waltham Mass.: Brandeis University Press, 2005), 162–181, and "Jewish Memory Between Exile and History," *Jewish Quarterly Review* 97 (Fall 2007): 530–543.

24. Susannah Heschel, *Abraham Geiger and the Jewish Jesus* (Chicago: University of Chicago Press, 1998), 3ff. See also the discussion in Reuven Michael, *Ha-ketivah ha-historit ha-Yehudit* (Jerusalem: Mosad Bialik, 1993), 279–300.

25. See Geiger's letters to Derenbourg from 30 September 1833, 23 February 1836, and 20 July 1841 (quotation) in Max Wiener, comp., *Abraham Geiger and Liberal Judaism: The Challenge of the Nineteenth Century*, translated by Ernst J. Schlochauer (Philadelphia: Jewish Publication Society, 1962), 83–84, 90.

26. Geiger, letter to Theodor Noeldecke, 1 December 1865, ibid., 128.

27. Heschel notes that Geiger "longed for something comparable in Judaism." Heschel, *Abraham Geiger and the Jewish Jesus*, 108. See Geiger's letter to Jacob Auerbach, 5 January 1837, in Wiener, comp., *Abraham Geiger and Liberal Judaism*, 103. Strauss himself modeled the use of scholarship as a tool of liberation from bias or naïveté in his controversial *Das Leben Jesu* (The Life of Jesus) of 1835. There he subjected the Gospels to critical scrutiny, casting their accounts of Jesus's life as mythical rather than factual. Through this book, the far-reaching "Historical Jesus" debate came into full public view in Europe

28. Wiener, comp., *Abraham Geiger and Liberal Judaism*, 156–157 (emphasis added).

29. Ibid., 168.

30. Geiger, letter to M. A. Stern, the German-Jewish mathematician, 14–16 November 1839, ibid., 108.

31. Wiener, comp., *Abraham Geiger and Liberal Judaism*, 155.

32. See Geiger's statement of 16 July 1845 in the rabbinic conference summary, *Protokolle und Aktenstuecke der zweiten Rabbiner-Versammlung* (Frankfurt am Main: E Ullmann, 1845), 18ff., excerpted in Mendes-Flohr and Reinharz, eds., *The Jew in the Modern World*, 203.

33. On the Hildesheimer Seminary, see David Ellenson, *Rabbi Esriel Hildesheimer and the Creation of a Modern Jewish Orthodoxy* (Tuscaloosa: University of Alabama Press, 1990), as well as David Ellenson and Richard Jacobs, "Scholarship and Faith: David Hoffmann and His Relation to Wissenschaft des Judentums," *Modern Judaism* 8 (1988): 27–40. See also

Assaf Yedidya, "Orthodox Reactions to 'Wissenschaft des Judentums,'" *Modern Judaism* 30 (2010): 69–94. On Orthodox historiography beyond Germany, see Haim Gertner, "Reshitah shel ketivah historit ortodoksit be-Mizraḥ Eropah: Ha-'arakhah meḥudeshet," *Tsiyon* 67, no. 3 (2002): 293–336; Nahum Karlinsky, *Historyah sheke-neged: "Igrot ha-ḥasidim me-Eretz-Yisra'el"; Ha-tekst veha-kontekst* (Jerusalem: Yad Ben-Zvi, 1998); Ada Rapoport-Albert, "Hagiography with Footnotes: Edifying Tales and the Writing of History in Hasidism," *History and Theory* 27 (1988): 119–159.

34. See Jawitz's introduction to the original 1895 edition reprinted in *Toldot Yisra'el*, 3rd ed. (Berlin: Yerah Etanim, 1924–1925), iv.

35. Ibid. For a helpful recent summary of Jawitz's life and work, see Assaf Yedidya, *Legadel tarbut 'Ivriyah: hayav u-mishnato shel Zeev Jawitz* (Jerusalem: Mosad Bialik, 2016). Jawitz, *Toldot Yisra'el*, vi. See Yedidya, *Legadel tarbut 'Ivriyah*, 86–88, as well as Brenner, *Prophets of the Past*, 158–159. Meanwhile, Graetz's biographer, Philipp Bloch, relates the story of Graetz's encounter with the older Zunz at the home of Michael Sachs in Berlin. When Zunz was told that Graetz was about to publish a new history, Zunz asked Graetz: "Another history of the Jews?" Graetz was said to respond, "Another history, but this time a *Jewish* history." See Bloch's memoir, based on Graetz's diaries, at the beginning of volume 6 of Heinrich Graetz, *History of the Jews* (Philadelphia: Jewish Publication Society, 1898), 60.

36. See Brenner, *Prophets of the Past*, 159. Yedidya notes the negative response of critical scholars, as well as Jawitz's difficulty in gaining readers among either secular or Orthodox audiences, in *Legadel tarbut 'Ivriyah*, 94–96, 189.

37. For a detailed analysis of the ArtScroll phenomenon in American Orthodox life, see Jeremy Stolow, *Orthodoxy by Design: Judaism, Print Politics, and the ArtScroll Revolution* (Berkeley: University of California Press, 2010), 8.

38. But see the accounts of the Christian scholars who are collected in Jean Delumeau, ed., *L'historien et la foi* (Paris: Fayard, 1996).

39. Berel Wein, *Triumph of Survival: The Story of the Jews in the Modern Era, 1650–1990* (Brooklyn, N.Y.: Shaar Press with Mesorah Publications, 1990), xi–xii. For Graetz's version of this quote, see Bloch in Graetz's *History of the Jews*, 60–61.

40. Yedidya, *Legadel tarbut 'Ivriyah*, 32–33.

41. Wein, *Triumph of Survival*, 43.

42. Brenner, *Prophets of the Past*, 204.

43. The Yale scholar John Lewis Gaddis has noted that historians embark on divergent paths by oppressing *and* liberating the past. Oppression comes about when the historian imposes an overarching structure on the evidence at hand. This imposition can be a sort of "prison from which there's neither escape nor reason nor appeal." But the historian, Gaddis hastened to add, also liberates in a variety of ways—from the ravages of amnesia, from the delusion of historical inevitability, and from the tyranny of a fixed interpretation of the past. See Gaddis, "Historians Both Oppress and Liberate the Past," *Yale Bulletin and Calendar,* 7 December 2001.

44. Leopold Zunz, "Vorrede," *Gottesdienstliche Vorträge der Juden, historisch entwickelt* (Berlin: A. Asher, 1832), reprinted in Zunz, *Gesammelte Schriften* (Berlin: Louis Lamm, 1919), 32–34.

45. Leopold Zunz, *Namen der Juden: Eine geschichtliche Untersuchung* (Leipzig: L. Fort, 1837). See also Schorsch, *Leopold Zunz,* 69–70.

46. Quoted in Amos Elon, *The Pity of It All: A Portrait of the German-Jewish Epoch, 1743–1933* (New York: Metropolitan Books, 2002), 163.

47. Baron wrote two exhaustive articles on the subject that could easily have made a single monograph. Curiously, Germany did not figure centrally for him, though he did note that at a later point German norms stifled the activist impulse of scholars. See Salo W. Baron, "The Revolution of 1848 and Jewish Scholarship, Part I: France, the United States and Italy," *Proceedings of the American Academy for Jewish Research* 18 (1948–1949): 1–66 (quotation, 4), and "The Revolution of 1848 and Jewish Scholarship, Part II: Austria," *Proceedings of the American Academy for Jewish Research* 20 (1951): 1–100.

48. Leon Pinsker, *Autoemancipation: Mahnruf an seine Stammesgenossen* (Berlin: Commissions-Verlag von W. Issleib, 1882).

49. The polyglot Dubnow published the essay originally in Russian in *Voskhod* 4–9 (1891): 1–91, and then in Hebrew as "Nahpesa ve-nakhkora" in *Ha-pardes* 1 (1892): 221–242. I have used here the English version, "Let Us Seek and Investigate," translated by Avner Greenberg, with the helpful historical introduction of Laura Jockusch in *Simon-Dubnow-Institut Jahrbuch* 7 (2008): 343–382.

50. Dubnow, "Let Us Seek and Investigate," 357, 360, 363.

51. The introduction has been translated by Koppel S. Pinson in his edition of Dubnow, *Nationalism and History* (Philadelphia: Jewish Publication Society, 1958), 339. See also Brenner, *Prophets of the Past,* 99–100.

52. Ahad Ha-am, "Tehiyat ha-ruah," *Ha-Shiloah* 10 (1902), reprinted in Ha-am, *'Al parashat derakhim* (Berlin: Jüdischer Verlag, 1921), 3: 121.

53. See Yosef Klausner, "Megamatenu," *Ha-Shiloah* 11 (1903): 9. On Klausner, see David N. Myers, *Re-Inventing the Jewish Past: European Jewish Intellectuals and the Zionist Return to History* (New York: Oxford University Press, 1995), 35, 93–99, and Brenner, *Prophets of the Past,* 160.

54. Gershom Scholem, "Kabbala at the Hebrew University," *Reconstructionist* 3, no. 10 (1937), 8–12.

55. Yitzhak Baer and Ben Zion Dinur, "Megamatenu," *Zion* 1 (1936): 1.

56. Yitzhak Baer, *Yisra'el ba-'amim* (Jerusalem: Mosad Bialik, 1955), 117.

57. Ben Zion Dinur (Dinaburg), *Yisra'el ba-Golah* (Tel Aviv: Devir and Mosad Bialik, 1958), vol. 1, book 1, 30–31 [Hebrew pagination].

58. So too did Baer, who ventured in the final sentence of *Galut* the idea that there is "a power that lifts the Jewish people out of the realm of all causal history." Yitzhak Baer, *Galut,* translated by Robert Warshow (New York: Schocken, 1947), 120.

59. Ben Zion Dinur, "Zekhutenu la-arets," in Mordechai Cohen, ed. *Perakim be-toldot Erets Yisra'el* (Jerusalem: Ministries of Education and Defense, 1981), 410–414. Ben-Gurion's comment is included in Shabtai Tevet, *Ben-Gurion and the Palestinian Arabs: From Peace to War* (Oxford: Oxford University Press, 1985), 97.

60. For example, Dr. Ziad Abu Amr, deputy prime minister of the Palestinian Authority (as of August 2013), made the case in 1995 for the Arabs' right to Jerusalem and Palestine without mentioning the presence of Jews in antiquity in "The Significance of Jerusalem: A Muslim Perspective," *Palestine-Israel Journal* 2, no. 2 (1995): at http://www.pij.org/details.php?id=646. More recently, Deputy Minister of Jerusalem Affairs Salwa Hadib declared on the Palestinian Authority television channel (24 May 2015) that "the Palestinian people has been present in it [Jerusalem] for thousands of years . . . centuries before the Jewish religion." The video clip can be found at http://www.palwatch.org/main.aspx?fi=157&doc_id=15297 (accessed on 28 August 2015).

61. For a careful reconstruction of the founding of YIVO, see Cecile Esther Kuznitz, *YIVO and the Making of Modern Jewish Culture: Scholarship for the Yiddish Nation* (New York: Cambridge University Press, 2014), 59ff.

62. On this pre-YIVO phase, see Barry Trachtenberg, *The Revolutionary Roots of Modern Yiddish, 1903–1917* (Syracuse, N.Y.: Syracuse University Press, 2008).

63. Nokhem Shtif, "Vegn a yidishn akademishn institute," in *Di organizatsye fun der yiddisher visnshaft* (Vilna: TSBK and VILBIG, 1925), 1, 24. See Kuznitz, *YIVO and the Making of Modern Jewish Culture,* 66.

64. Shtif, writing under his penname Bal-dimyen, "Der yiddisher visn-shaftlekher institute, a yor arbet," *Varshever shrift* (1926–1927): 2–3, quoted in Kuznitz, *YIVO and the Making of Modern Jewish Culture*, 64.

65. A locus classicus is Joan Scott's *Gender and the Politics of History* (New York: Columbia University Press, 1988).

66. Gerda Lerner, "Why History Matters," in Lerner, *Why History Matters: Life and Thought* (New York: Oxford University Press, 1997), 206–207.

67. Ibid., 210–211.

68. Ibid., 5.

69. Paula E. Hyman, "Immigrant Women and Consumer Protest: The New York City Kosher Meat Boycott of 1902," *American Jewish History* 70, no. 1 (1980): 91.

70. Paula E. Hyman, "Gender and the Immigrant Jewish Experience in the United States," in Judith R. Baskin, ed., *Jewish Women in Historical Perspective* (Detroit: Wayne State University Press, 1991), 312.

71. Paula E. Hyman, *Gender and Assimilation in Modern Jewish History: The Roles and Representations of Women* (Seattle: University of Washington Press, 1995), 5ff.

72. Paula E. Hyman, introduction to Puah Rakovsky, *My Life as a Radical Jewish Woman: Memoirs of a Zionist Feminist in Poland,* translated by Paula E. Hyman (Bloomington: Indiana University Press, 2002), 3.

Chapter 2
History as Consolation

1. Yosef Hayim Yerushalmi, "Toward a History of Jewish Hope," in David N. Myers and Alexander Kaye, eds., *The Faith of Fallen Jews: Yosef Hayim Yerushalmi and the Writing of Jewish History* (Hanover, N.H.: Brandeis University Press, 2014), 315.

2. It is curious that both Yerushalmi and his teacher Salo W. Baron used a similar term, although with reference to different time periods and understandings. For Yerushalmi, Jews in earlier eras invoked a "midrash of history" to transform the past into "a text, capable of interpretation through a hermeneutic that flowed naturally and unselfconsciously out of the fundamental premises of Israelite faith." Yerushalmi, "Toward a History of Jewish Hope," 313. Meanwhile, in his late methodological reflections, Baron declared, with an eye on the present, that the study of the past might "serve as a sort of new historical *midrash* and help answer some of the most perplexing questions of the present and the future." Salo

W. Baron, *The Contemporary Relevance of History* (New York: Columbia University Press, 1986), 98.

3. The English scholar Rivkah Zim has written a comprehensive account of the long tradition of authors who turn to writing while imprisoned as a form of consolation. She analyzes how they used various forms of literature to defend their values against persecution, to cast an image of themselves for posterity, and to bear witness after the fact to the excesses that they and others had experienced. Rivkah Zim, *Consolations of Writing: Literary Strategies of Resistance from Boethius to Primo Levi* (Princeton: Princeton University Press, 2014), 16–18. Boethius spent the last year of his life in prison after being apprehended on a flimsily constructed charge of conspiracy in Verona. Knowing that his punishment would be death, he wrote *The Consolation of Philosophy,* which became one of the most widely disseminated and copied Latin texts of all time—and surely one of the most popular works ever on a philosophical theme. Employing the framework of a Platonic dialogue, Boethius stages a sustained dialogue between "Boethius" and Lady Philosophy, who dispenses wisdom about the nature and conduct of life. True contentment, Lady Philosophy ordains, cannot be measured in material wealth; it resides rather in mental and moral virtue. She reminds Boethius that Fortune can and often does abandon individuals, but ultimately it cannot undermine the essential goodness of human nature. See *The Consolation of Philosophy,* translated by W. V. Cooper (Ex-Classics Project, 2009), at http://www.exclassics .com/consol/consol.pdf.

4. Frederick Tupper, "The Consolation of History: An After Dinner Speech at the Annual Banquet of the Vermont Commandery of the Loyal Legion of the United States, May 11, 1920," https://openlibrary.org/books/ OL23415182M/The_consolation_of_history (accessed on 8 August 2014).

5. David G. Roskies, ed., *Literature of Destruction: Jewish Responses to Catastrophe* (Philadelphia: Jewish Publication Society, 1988), 3, 5. See also David G. Roskies, *Against the Apocalypse: Responses to Catastrophe in Modern Jewish Culture* (Cambridge: Harvard University Press, 1984), and Alan Mintz, *Hurban: Responses to Catastrophe in Hebrew Literature* (New York: Columbia University Press, 1984).

6. Paul Fussell, *The Great War and Modern Memory* (New York: Oxford University Press, 1975), 247.

7. See Roskies, *Against the Apocalypse,* 10. See the new edition with an admiring and critical introduction by the Yale historian of World War I Jay Winter, Paul Fussell, *The Great War and Modern Memory* (New York: Oxford University Press, 2013).

8. See "How the Brain Creates New Neural Pathways," http://www .whatisneuroplasticity.com/pathways.php (accessed on 4 October 2015). For a more detailed scientific discussion of neuroplasticity and memory, see Federico Bermúdez-Rattoni, ed., *Neural Plasticity and Memory: From Genes to Brain Imaging* (Boca Raton, Fla.: CRC Press/Taylor and Francis, 2007).

9. Maurice Halbwachs, *The Collective Memory* (New York: Harper and Row, 1980), 48.

10. Eviatar Zerubavel, *Time Maps: Collective Memory and the Social Shape of the Past* (Chicago: University of Chicago Press, 2003), 28. See also Yehuda Kurtzer, *Shuva: The Future of the Jewish Past* (Waltham, Mass.: Brandeis University Press, 2012), 20–22.

11. Jay Winter and Emmanuel Sivan prefer the term "collective remembrance" to "collective memory." As they define it, "Collective remembrance is public recollection. It is the act of gathering bits and pieces of the past, and joining them together in public. The 'public' is the group that produces, expresses, and consumes it. What they create is not a cluster of individual memories; the whole is greater than the sum of the parts." See Winter and Sivan, eds., *War and Remembrance in the Twentieth Century* (Cambridge: Cambridge University Press, 1999), 6.

12. All translations of the Bible are from the 1985 Jewish Publication Society edition, *Tanakh: The Holy Scriptures* (Philadelphia: Jewish Publication Society, 1985).

13. See Ricouer's meditation "On Consolation" in Alasdair MacIntyre and Paul Ricoeur, *The Religious Significance of Atheism* (New York: Columbia University Press, 1969), 89.

14. Flavius Josephus, *Against Apion,* in *The Works of Flavius Josephus,* translated by William Whiston, available at http://www.ccel.org/ccel/ josephus/works/files/apion-1.htm.

15. For competing perspectives on the Chronicles' veracity, see Ivan Marcus, "From Politics to Martyrdom: Shifting Paradigms in the Hebrew Narratives of the 1096 Crusader Riots," *Prooftexts* 2 (1982): 40–52, Robert Chazan, *God, Humanity, and History: The Hebrew First Crusade Narratives* (Berkeley: University of California Press, 2000), and Jeremy Cohen, *Sanctifying the Name of God: Jewish Martyrs and Jewish Memories of the First Crusade* (Philadelphia: University of Pennsylvania Press, 2006). To be sure, debates over the genre, utility, and function of the medieval chronicle are not restricted to Hebrew versions. The Christian Latin chronicle is the subject of a rich body of scholarship that has prompted the formation of a learned society entirely devoted to studying it. See the Medieval Chronicle Society website: http://medievalchronicle.org/.

16. Shlomo Eidelberg, ed., *The Jews and the Crusaders: The Hebrew Chronicles of the First and Second Crusades* (Madison: University of Wisconsin Press, 1977), 25.

17. Ibid., 33, 49, 93.

18. Marcus, "From Politics to Martyrdom," 43.

19. In the controversial argument of Yisrael Yuval, the vengeance-driven impulse of Jewish victims of the Crusades and their descendants—with its focus on avenging the blood of the martyrs—was absorbed and transformed by contemporaneous Christians into the blood libel charge that is first raised against Jews in the twelfth century. See Yuval, "Hanakam veha-kelalah, ha-dat veha-'alilah mi'alilot kedoshim le-'alilot dam," *Zion* 58 (1993): 33–90.

20. In addition to the work of Marcus, Chazan, and Cohen cited in note 15, above, see Yosef Hayim Yerushalmi, *Zakhor: Jewish History and Jewish Memory* (Seattle: University of Washington Press, 1982), chap. 2, and Eva Haverkamp, *Hebräische Berichte über die Judenverfolgungen während des Ersten Kreuzzugs* (Hebrew Accounts of the Persecutions of the Jews During the First Crusade) (Hannover: Hahnsche Buchhandlung, 2005).

21. For an important analysis of an Ashkenazic martyrological sensibility extending from 1096 to 1648–1649, see Yehezkel (Edward) Fram, "Ben TaTNaV (1096) le-TaH/TaT (1648–49): 'iyun mi-hadash," *Zion* 61 (1996): 159–182.

22. See Mintz, *Hurban*, 89. For an important exchange of views on differences between Ashkenazic and Sephardic visions of past and future, see Gerson D. Cohen, "Messianic Postures of Ashkenazim and Sephardim," *Studies of the Leo Baeck Institute*, edited by M. Kreutzberger (New York: Unger, 1967), 115–156, and Elisheva Carlebach, "Between History and Hope: Jewish Messianism in Ashkenaz and Sepharad," Third Annual Lecture of the Victor Selmanowitz Chair of Jewish History, Touro College, New York, 1998.

23. Well before Usque's account, the twelfth-century Spanish scholar Abraham ibn Daud wrote of the "great consolations" that issued from the prophetic parables about the history of Second Temple kings. See Gerson D. Cohen, *The Book of Tradition (Sefer Ha-Qabbalah) by Abraham ibn Daud* (Philadelphia: Jewish Publication Society, 1967), 14 (Hebrew section). I thank Michael A. Meyer for this reference.

24. Samuel Usque, *Consolation for the Tribulations of Israel,* edited and translated by Martin A. Cohen (Philadelphia: Jewish Publication Society, 1977). See also Yosef Hayim Yerushalmi, "A Jewish Classic in the

Portuguese Language," introduction to Usque, *Consolação ás Tribulações de Israel*, (Lisbon: Fundação Calouste Gulbenkian, 1989).

25. Usque, *Consolation for the Tribulations of Israel*, 227–232.

26. Cf. Azariah de' Rossi, *The Light of the Eyes*, translated and introduced by Joanna Weinberg (New Haven: Yale University Press, 2001), and Jeremy Cohen, *A Historian in Exile: Solomon ibn Verga, "Shevet Yehudah," and the Jewish-Christian Encounter* (Philadelphia: University of Pennsylvania Press, 2017). Cohen notes the ways in which ibn Verga adumbrates a more modern approach to history: his idea of the "natural cause" as an explanatory model, his interest in economic and social factors, and a measure of skepticism toward religion. Cohen, *A Historian in Exile*, 5.

27. Salo W. Baron, "Ghetto and Emancipation: Shall We Revise the Traditional View?" *Menorah Journal* 14 (June 1928): 515–526. See David Engel, *Historians of the Jews and the Holocaust* (Stanford, Calif.: Stanford University Press, 2010), esp. chap. 1, "Negating Lachrymosity."

28. On the relationship between premodern and modern Jewish historical writers, see David N. Myers, *Resisting History: Historicism and Its Discontents in German-Jewish Thought* (Princeton: Princeton University Press, 2003), 16–25. See also Karl Löwith, *Meaning in History: The Theological Implications of the Philosophy of History* (Chicago: University of Chicago Press, 1949), who, regarded modern teleologies of history as a misguided attempt to secularize fundamentally religious perspective. Seventeen years later, Hans Blumenberg challenged Löwith's stance in *The Legitimacy of the Modern Age*, arguing that Löwith's periodization was mistaken since the attempted secularization had already occurred in the Middle Ages. Hans Blumenberg, *The Legitimacy of the Modern Age* (Cambridge: MIT Press, 1985). For an exposition of the contours and stakes of the debate, see Stephen A. McKnight, "The Legitimacy of the Modern Age: The Lowith-Blumenberg Debate in Light of Recent Scholarship," *Political Science Reviewer* (Spring 1990): 177–195.

29. Simon Rawidowicz, one of Krochmal's most important modern expositors, for example, points to the influence of Gotthold Ephraim Lessing, Herder, and especially Vico in his introduction to the 1924 critical edition of *More nevukhe ha-zeman*. See the revised second edition of Rawidowicz, ed. *Kitve Rabi Nachman Krochmal* (London: Ararat, 1971), 117, esp. n. 4. In contrast, Krochmal's later biographer Jay Harris maintains that establishing the thinker's intellectual influences is "hopeless." See Jay M. Harris, *Nachman Krochmal: Guiding the Perplexed of the Modern Age* (New York: New York University Press, 1993), 125.

30. Shlomo Avineri, "The Fossil and the Phoenix: Hegel and Krochmal

on the Jewish Volksgeist," in Robert L. Perkins, ed. *History and System: Hegel's Philosophy of History* (Albany: State University of New York Press, 1984), 47–72. Vico, for his part, believed that Jewish history transcended the cycles to which other nations were subjected. See Adam Sutcliffe, *Judaism and Enlightenment* (Cambridge: Cambridge University Press, 2003), 77ff.

31. Nachman Krochmal, *More nevukhe ha-zeman* in Rawidowicz, ed., *Kitve Rabi Nahman Krochmal*, 40. See also Harris, *Nachman Krochmal*, 126–155, as well as Salo W. Baron, *The Contemporary Relevance of History: A Study in Approaches and Methods* (New York: Columbia University Press, 1986), 6, and Yehudah Mirsky, *Rav Kook: Mystic in a Time of Revolution* (New Haven: Yale University Press, 2014), 79–80.

32. See Ismar Schorsch, *From Text to Context: The Turn to History in Modern Judaism* (Hanover, N.H.: Brandeis University Press, 1994), 6 and Michael A. Meyer, "Two Persistent Tensions Within *Wissenschaft des Judentums*," *Modern Judaism* 24 (2004): 105–119. See also Sven Erik-Rose, *Jewish Philosophical Politics in Germany, 1789–1848* (Waltham, Mass.: Brandeis University Press, 2014), 48ff, as well as Myers, "The Ideology of *Wissenschaft des Judentums*" in Daniel H. Frank and Oliver Leaman, eds., *History of Jewish Philosophy* (London: Routledge, 1997), 706–720. In addition, see Michael Brenner, *Prophets of the Past: Interpreters of Jewish History*, translated by Steven Rendall (Princeton: Princeton University Press, 2010), 9–11, and Nils H. Roemer, *Jewish Scholarship and Culture in Nineteenth-Century Germany: Between History and Faith* (Madison: University of Wisconsin Press, 2005), 15ff.

33. Enterprises such as the Historische Commission für Geschichte der Juden in Deutschland (1885) and the Gesellschaft zur Förderung der Wissenschaft des Judentums (1902)—and their companion projects such as Germania Judaica and the Gesamtarchiv der deutschen Juden—were designed to preserve, and publicize the relevance of, Jewish history in Germany. On the commemoration and memorialization of history by German Jews, see Jacques Ehrenfreund, *Les juifs berlinois à la Belle Époque* (Paris: Presses Universitaires de France, 2000).

34. Pierre Nora, introduction to *Les Lieux de mémoire*, "Between Memory and History: *Les Lieux de Mémoire*," which was reprinted in *Representations* 26 (Spring 1989): 7.

35. Heinrich Graetz played that role in the midst of the Berlin *Antisemitismusstreit* in 1879–1880, pushing back against the menacing claims of the German nationalist historian Heinrich von Treitschke that Jews (and Graetz, in particular) were incapable of loyalty to their homeland.

See Michael A. Meyer, "Heinrich Graetz and Heinrich von Treitschke: A Comparison of Their Historical Images of the Modern Jew," *Modern Judaism* 6 (February 1986): 1–11.

36. For example, Dubnow, who at an early point in his career criticized Graetz for his tendency to depict Jewish history as a lugubrious "history of suffering," went on to describe the Crusades as "the era of mass slaughter." Simon Dubnow, *Weltgeschichte des jüdischen Volkes*, vol. 4 (Berlin: Jüdischer Verlag, 1926), 271. For a discussion of Dubnow and others, see David N. Myers, "'*Mehabevin et ha-tsarot*': Crusade Memories and Modern Jewish Martyrologies," *Jewish History* 13, no. 2 (Fall 1999): 50–64.

37. Siegmund Salfeld, ed., *Das Martyrologium des Nürnberger Memorbuches* (Berlin: Leonhard Simion, 1898), vi. See also Myers, "'*Mehabevin et ha-tsarot*,'" 56.

38. See Zeev Jawitz, *Sefer Toldot Yisra'el*, rev. ed. (Tel Aviv: Ahi'ever, 1933–1934), 11: 53–54. Jawitz's adulatory tone toward martyrdom was notably lacking in a pair of rather dry scholarly editions of materials related to the Jewish experience during the Crusades that appeared in 1892 and 1898 under the sponsorship of the Historische Commission für Geschichte der Juden in Deutschland.

39. Salo W. Baron, *A Social and Religious History of the Jews*, vol. 2 (New York: Columbia University Press, 1937), 31.

40. Shimon Bernfeld, *Sefer ha-dema'ot: me'ora'ot ha-gezerot veha-redifot veha-shemadot*, 3 vols. (Berlin: Hotsa'ot Eschkol, 1923–1926), 1: 147.

41. Ibid., 1: 6. See also Myers, "'*Mehabevin et ha-tsarot*,'" 57–60.

42. Baron, "Ghetto and Emancipation," 526.

43. Bernfeld, *Sefer ha-dema'ot*, 3: 5, 8.

44. Simon Dubnow, "Sod ha-kiyum ve-hok ha-kiyum shel 'am Yisra'el" (The Secret of Survival—and the Law of Survival—of the Jewish People), *He-'atid* 7 (1923): 116.

45. Simon Dubnow, introduction to *Antisemitism un pogromen in Ukraine, 1917–1918: tsu der geshikhte fun Ukrainish-Yidishe batsihungen* (Berlin: Mizreh-Yidishn historishn arkhiv, 1923), 9, 15. À propos revenge, a traditional Jewish imprecation conveys a sense of vengeance directed at violent enemies of Israel by calling for "their names and memories to be blotted out [forever]." The measure of succor that it provides, laced with bitterness though it may be, is distinct from the unmistakably Christian impulse, identified by Paul Ricoeur, that regards consolation as "deliverance *from* revenge." MacIntyre and Ricoeur, *The Religious Significance of Atheism*, 95.

46. Ismar Schorsch, "German Judaism: From Confession to Culture," in Arnold Paucker et al., eds., *Die Juden im Nationalsozialistischen*

Deutschland: The Jews in Nazi Germany, 1933–1943 (Tübingen: Mohr Siebeck, 1986), 68.

47. For a discussion of the series (and a list of its titles), see Renate Evers, "Die 'Schocken-Bücherei' in den Nachlasssammlungen des Leo Baeck Institutes New York," *Medaon* 14 (2014), accessed at http://www.medaon.de/pdf/MEDAON_14_Evers.pdf.

48. Naar explores this cohort in his impressive study *Jewish Salonica Between the Ottoman Empire and Modern Greece* (Stanford: Stanford University Press, 2016), 191, 209.

49. Samuel D. Kassow, *Who Will Write Our History? Emanuel Ringelblum and the Oyneg Shabes Archive* (Bloomington: Indiana University Press, 2007).

50. See Ringelblum's essay, "O.S. (Oyneg Shabbes), December 1944, in Joseph Kermish, ed., *To Live with Honor and Die with Honor! . . . : Selected Documents from the Warsaw Ghetto Underground Archives "O.S."* (Jerusalem: Yad Vashem, 1986), 4. Ringelblum's colleague was Hersh Wasser, who recorded them. See Kassow, *Who Will Write Our History?*, 387.

51. Ringelblum wrote in 1942: "Comprehensiveness was the main principle of our work. Objectivity was the second. We endeavoured to convey the whole truth, no matter how bitter, and we presented faithful unadorned pictures." Kermish, ed., *To Live with Honor,* 9.

52. See Kermish, ed., *To Live with Honor,* 10.

53. For a superb discussion of the origins of the concept in the work of the Yiddish historian Mark Dworzecki in 1946, see Mark L. Smith, "The Yiddish Historians and the Struggle for a Jewish History of the Holocaust" (Ph.D. diss., University of California, Los Angeles, 2016), 342ff. See also the extensive discussion of the term by the notable historian Yehuda Bauer in *Rethinking the Holocaust* (New Haven: Yale University Press, 2002), 119–166.

54. Selma Stern, *The Court Jew: A Contribution to the History of the Period of Absolutism in Central Europe* (Philadelphia: Jewish Publication Society, 1950), viii, 267.

55. Ibid., xv.

Chapter 3
History as Witness

1. Thucydides, *History of the Peloponnesian War,* translated by Richard Crawley, 1: 22. Available at http://people.ucalgary.ca/~vandersp/Courses/texts/thucydi1.html#Top. All quotations are from this edition.

2. See Lawrence Douglas, *The Memory of Judgment: Making Law and History in the Trials of the Holocaust* (New Haven: Yale University Press, 2001). On the etymology of "martyr," see http://www.etymonline.com/index.php?term=martyr&allowed_in_frame=0. Accessed on 23 September 2014.

3. The Polish Nobel laureate Czesław Miłosz gave voice to this ideal in his published Charles Eliot Norton Lectures at Harvard, in which he related, "I have titled this book *The Witness of Poetry* not because we witness it, but because it witnesses us." Czesław Miłosz, *The Witness of Poetry* (Cambridge: Harvard University Press, 1983), 4.

4. Primo Levi, *The Reawakening*, trans. Stuart Woolf (New York: Collier, 1987), 196. The second volume of Levi's memoir was published in Italian as *La Trega* in 1963. Michael Tager notes that a "demand for justice underlies Levi's witness" in "Primo Levi and the Language of Witness," *Criticism* 35 (Spring 1993): 265–288 (quote at 281).

5. Carlo Ginzburg, "Just One Witness," in Saul Friedlander, ed. *Probing the Limits of Representation: Nazism and the "Final Solution"* (Cambridge: Harvard University Press, 1992), 82–96.

6. Carlo Ginzburg, *The Judge and the Historian: Marginal Notes on a Late-Twentieth-Century Miscarriage of Justice,* translated by Anthony Shugaar (London: Verso, 1999), 17.

7. Ibid., 117–120.

8. Robert M. Cover, "Nomos and Narrative," *Harvard Law Review* 97, no. 4 (1983–1984): 9, 11.

9. Robert M. Cover, "Folktales of Justice: Tales of Jurisdiction," *Capital University Law Review* 14, no. 179 (1984–1985): 189–190.

10. Annette Wieviorka, *The Era of the Witness,* translated by Jared Stark (Ithaca: Cornell University Press, 2006), 1. For an exhaustive account of Yiddish historians during and after the war, see Mark L. Smith, "Yiddish Historians and the Struggle for a Jewish History of the Holocaust" (Ph.D. diss., University of California, Los Angeles, 2016).

11. Dubnow's first essay about the pogrom, "A Historic Moment" (May 1903), appears in English in his *Nationalism and History: Essays on Old and New Judaism,* ed. Koppel S. Pinson (Philadelphia: Jewish Publication Society, 1958), 192–199. For background on Dubnow's work around Kishinev, as well as a wider discussion of the project of khurbn-forshung, see Laura Jockusch's important *Collect and Record! Jewish Holocaust Documentation in Early Postwar Europe* (New York: Oxford University Press, 2015), 18ff., as well as her article "Chroniclers of Catastrophe: History Writing as a Jewish Response to Persecution Before and After

the Holocaust," in David Bankier and Dan Michman, eds., *Holocaust Historiography in Context: Emergence, Challenges, Polemics and Achievements* (Jerusalem: Yad Vashem, 2008), 138–145.

12. Alexandra Garbarini, "Power in Truth Telling: Jewish Testimonial Strategies Before the Shoah," in Jason Coy et al., eds., *Kinship, Community, and Self: Essays in Honor of David Warren Sabean* (New York: Berghahn, 2014), 174. See also Jockusch, "Chroniclers of Catastrophe," 148–155.

13. Leo Koch, "Professor Shimen Dubnov un zayn barbarishe talmid," *Yidishe Kultur* 7 (May 1945): 39. See also Ilya Ehrenberg and Vasily Grossman, *The Complete Black Book of Russian Jewry,* translated and edited by David Patterson (New Brunswick, N.J.: Transaction, 2009), 387–388.

14. Koppel S. Pinson records this quote in Dubnow, *Nationalism and History,* 39. His report is based on the near-contemporaneous account of Hillel Melamed, whose father, Hirsch, was a friend of Dubnow's in Riga, "Vo azoy di nazis hobn dermordet Prof. Sh. Dubnow," *Di tsukunft* 51 (1946): 320–321. See also the work by Dubnow's daughter Sophie Dubnov-Erlich, *The Life and Work of S. J. Dubnow* (Bloomington: Indiana University Press, 1991).

15. Samuel D. Kassow, *Who Will Write Our History? Emanuel Ringelblum, the Warsaw Ghetto, and the Oyneg Shabes Archive* (Bloomington: Indiana University Press, 2007), 213.

16. Vladimir Petrović has studied the function of historical witnessing in his dissertation, "Historians as Expert Witnesses in the Age of Extremes." He notes the presence of historians at the trials of Alfred Dreyfus and Émil Zola, as well as in the libel case directed against the historian Heinrich Friedjung in the early twentieth century. See Petrović, "Historians as Expert Witnesses in the Age of Extremes" (Ph.D. diss., Central European University, Budapest, 2008), 60–64.

17. Ulrich Sieg titles his chapter devoted to the case "The Talmud on Trial" in his *Germany's Prophet: Paul de Lagarde and the Origins of Modern Antisemitism,* translated by Linda Ann Marianello (Waltham, Mass.: Brandeis University Press, 2013), 202–214. Nils Roemer observes that it was not simply that Judaism was on the defensive in Germany at that time; rather, it was a case of "*Wissenschaft* on trial." See Nils Roemer, *Jewish Scholarship and Culture in Nineteenth-Century Germany: Between History and Faith* (Madison: University of Wisconsin Press, 2005), 83ff. See also Barnet Hartston, *Sensationalizing the Jewish Question: Anti-Semitic Trials and the Press in the Early German Empire* (Leiden: Brill, 2015), 215.

18. An interesting hybrid of the work of textual and courtroom witnessing may be commissions of inquiry, established in the wake of tragedies or momentous events in order to determine responsibility, prevent repetition, and set in place a public memory for the future. For a probing discussion of the place of commissions of inquiry in Israeli society and their efforts to forge public memory, see Nadav G. Molchadsky, "History in the Public Courtroom: Commissions of Inquiry and Struggles over the History and Memory of Israeli Traumas," (Ph.D. diss., University of California, Los Angeles, 2015).

19. I thank Magda Teter for her comments on a version of this chapter presented at a conference at Cardozo Law School, 25 September 2016. See also John Hope Franklin, *Mirror to America: The Autobiography of John Hope Franklin* (New York: Farrar, Straus and Giroux, 2005), 156–158.

20. The discrimination case was initially brought by the Equal Employment Opportunities Commission (EEOC) against Sears, Roebuck & Company in 1973. The EEOC maintained that Sears favored white men over women for higher-paying commission sales jobs. Testifying on behalf of the defense was Rosalind Rosenberg of Barnard College; Alice Kessler-Harris, then of Hofstra University, served as an expert witness on behalf of the plaintiffs. Rosenberg argued that Sears was not to blame for differential employment patterns; rather, she argued, women and men have different expectations and values in choosing jobs. Kessler-Harris, for her part, maintained that women's choices in the job market were constrained by the opportunities presented to them—and that the case at hand amounted to discrimination. These competing views with the quotations are reported by Samuel G. Freedman in "Of History and Politics: Bitter Feminist Debate," *New York Times*, 6 June 1986, accessed at http://www.nytimes.com/1986/06/06/nyregion/of-history-and-politics-bitter-feminist-debate.html?pagewanted=all. See also Ruth Milkman, "Women's History and the Sears Case," *Feminist Studies* 12, no. 2 (1986): 375–400, as well Katherine Jellison, "History in the Courtroom: The Sears Case in Perspective," *Public Historian* 9 (Autumn 1987): 9–19.

21. Kelly Scott Johnson, "Scholem Schwarzbard: Biography of a Jewish Assassin" (Ph.D. diss., Harvard University, 2012), 180.

22. Saul S. Friedman, *Pogromchik: The Assassination of Simon Petlura* (New York: Hart, 1976), 289. For amplification on the Schwarzbard trial, see David Engel, "Being Lawful in a Lawless World: The Trial of Scholem Schwarzbard and the Defense of East European Jews," *Simon Dubnow Institute Yearbook* 5 (2006): 83–97.

23. It is commonly thought that the use of expert witnesses in court,

usually scientific rather than historical, commenced in the English case of *Folkes v. Chadd* in 1782. See Keith J. B. Rix, "Expert Evidence and the Courts: 1. The History of Expert Evidence," *Advances in Psychiatric Treatment* 5 (1999): 71.

24. This was the formulation of an American prosecutor, the German-born Jew Robert Kempner, Quoted in Buruma, *Wages of Guilt,* 144–145. See Douglas, *The Memory of Judgment,* 2. On Tcherikower's prominence, see Garbarini, "Power in Truth Telling," 177.

25. See the divergent perspectives on the role of Institute of Jewish Affairs in the Nuremberg prosecution offered by Michael R. Marrus, "A Jewish Lobby at Nuremberg: Jacob Robinson and the Institute of Jewish Affairs, 1945–46," *Cardozo Law Review* 27, no. 4 (2006): 1651–1665, and Boaz Cohen, "Dr. Jacob Robinson, the Institute of Jewish Affairs and the Elusive Jewish Voice in Nuremberg," *Holocaust and Justice: Representation and Historiography of the Holocaust in Post-War Trials* (Jerusalem: Yad Vashem and Berghahn Books, 2011), 81–100.

26. Donald Bloxham, "Jewish Witnesses in War Crimes Trials of the Postwar Era," in Bankier and Michman, eds., *Holocaust Historiography in Context,* 542.

27. Ibid.

28. Quoted in Cohen, "Dr. Jacob Robinson," 94.

29. These are the key protagonists in Smith's "The Yiddish Historians and the Struggle for a Jewish History of the Holocaust."

30. See Laura Jockusch's important book on historical commissions, *Collect and Record!,* as well as the new volume edited by Jockusch and Gabriel Finder, *Jewish Honor Courts: Revenge, Retribution, and Reconciliation in Europe and Israel After the Holocaust* (Detroit: Wayne State University Press, 2015). See also the important dissertation by Rivka Brot, "Ben kehilah li-medinah: mishpatehem shel meshatfe pe'ulah Yehudim 'im Natsim" (Ph.D. diss., Tel Aviv University, 2015).

31. Jean-François Lyotard, *The Differend: Phrases in Dispute,* translated by Georges Van Den Abbeele (Minneapolis: University of Minnesota Press, 1983), 55.

32. See Mathew Turner, "Historians as Expert Witnesses: How Do Holocaust Perpetrator Trials Shape Historiography?" *Alfred Deakin Research Institute Working Paper 22* (November 2011): 5–12.

33. For example, Baron declared that "it is clear that Emancipation has not brought the Golden Age." Salo W. Baron "Ghetto and Emancipation: Shall We Revise the Traditional View?" *Menorah Journal* 14 (June 1928): 526.

34. According to Hanna Yablonka, "Baron's optimism, so misplaced, had nothing in common with the pessimism that imbued the whole history of Zionism, which saw in Diaspora existence a condition that would end in catastrophe." Yablonka, *The State of Israel vs. Adolf Eichmann,* translated by Ora Cummings (New York: Schocken, 2004), 101. Nonetheless, Hausner reported that despite Ben-Gurion's preference, he chose Baron over Shazar because he wanted an expert witness who would stick to the facts and not be excessively emotional, as he feared Shazar would be. Gideon Hausner, *Mishpat Yerushalayim* (Tel Aviv: Bet lohame ha-geta'ot and Ha-kibuts ha-me'uchad, 1980), 299.

35. Pinchas Rosen to Benjamin Eliav, 26 December 1960, unnamed translator, Salo W. Baron Archives, Box 65, Folder 5, Stanford University. The Zionist concept to which Rosen makes indirect reference is *shelilat ha-golah,* or negation of the Diaspora.

36. Hausner stated that he was seeking someone who could "relate in general fashion the story of European Jewry, what was before the Shoah and what remained after it." Hausner, *Mishpat Yerushalayim,* 299, 327.

37. Yablonka, *The State of Israel vs. Adolf Eichmann,* 102. Baron testimony transcript, session 12, part 6, *The Nizkor Project:* "The Trial of Adolf Eichmann," http://www.nizkor.org/hweb/people/e/eichmann-adolf/transcripts/Sessions/Session-012-06.html. See also Robert Liberles, *Salo Wittmayer Baron: Architect of Jewish History* (New York: New York University Press, 1995), 330.

38. Baron testimony transcript, session 12, part 7, *The Nizkor Project:* "The Trial of Adolf Eichmann," http://www.nizkor.org/hweb/people/e/eichmann-adolf/transcripts/Sessions/Session-012-07.html.

39. Baron testimony transcript, session 12, part 6, *The Nizkor Project,* http://www.nizkor.org/hweb/people/e/eichmann-adolf/transcripts/Sessions/Session-012-06.html. For a minor modification of the English translation (changing "feat" to "feature"), see the Hebrew transcript at http://index.justice.gov.il/Subjects/EichmannWritten/volume/Vol1_p114.pdf.

40. Baron testimony transcript, session 13, part 2, *The Nizkor Project,* http://www.nizkor.org/hweb/people/e/eichmann-adolf/transcripts/Sessions/Session-013-02.html. See also Liberles, *Salo Wittmayer Baron,* 333–334.

41. Baron testimony transcript, session 12, part 7, *The Nizkor Project.*

42. Yablonka, *The State of Israel vs. Adolf Eichmann,* 104.

43. It does not seem the case, as Yablonka concludes, that Baron's testimony "came under attack from all quarters." Ibid., 103. See, for exam-

ple, the reports on Baron's testimony on 25 April 1961 in the Revisionist Zionist party newspaper, *Herut,* "Yeshivat ha-boker: Prof. Baron megolel bifne bet ha-mishpat et terumat Yahadut Eropa le-Yisra'el ve-'olam," and by G. Kressel, "Shalom Baron 'im 'eduto be-mishpat Eichmann," *Davar,* 25 April 1961. See also the companion pieces "Eichmann Court Hears Historian" and "Top Jewish Historian: Salo Wittmayer Baron," *New York Times,* 25 April 1961. Liberles reports on additional journalistic commentary in *Salo Wittmayer Baron,* 334–335.

44. Liberles, *Salo Wittmayer Baron,* 323.

45. Hannah Arendt, *Eichmann in Jerusalem: A Report on the Banality of Evil* (New York: Viking, 1963), 19.

46. Ibid., 9–10.

47. Bettina Stangneth, *Eichmann Before Jerusalem: The Unexamined Life of a Mass Murderer* (New York: Vintage, 2015).

48. Douglas, *The Memory of Judgment,* 260.

49. See Douglas's discussion of "heroic memory" ibid., 160–173.

50. See Jacques Derrida's interview with Poliakov, in "Humanity, Nationality, Bestiality," in Elisabeth Weber, *Questioning Judaism: Interviews by Elisabeth Weber* (Stanford, Calif.: Stanford University Press, 2004), 96–97.

51. Richard J. Evans, "History, Memory and the Law: The Historian as Expert Witness," *History and Theory* 41 (October 2002): 338.

52. Ian Buruma, *The Wages of Guilt: Memories of War in Germany and Japan* (New York: Farrar, Straus and Giroux, 1994), 142.

53. Robert O. Paxton, "The Trial of Maurice Papon," *New York Review of Books,* 16 December 1999, available at http://www.nybooks.com/articles/1999/12/16/the-trial-of-maurice-papon/#fnr-22. See also Paxton, *Vichy France: Old Guard and New Order, 1940–1944* (New York: Knopf, 1972). Paxton reflected on his work as witness in Elisabeth Bumiller," A Historian Defends His Leap from Past to Present," *New York Times,* 31 January 1998, available at http://www.nytimes.com/1998/01/31/books/a-historian-defends-his-leap-from-past-to-present.html.

54. Richard J. Evans, *Lying About Hitler: History, Holocaust, and the David Irving Trial* (New York: Basic, 2001), 7.

55. Deborah E. Lipstadt, *History on Trial: My Day in Court with David Irving* (New York: Ecco, 2005), 208.

56. Evans, *Lying About Hitler,* 227.

57. Lipstadt, *History on Trial,* 275.

58. Evans, *Lying About Hitler,* 2, 35, 265. See also Richard J. Evans, *In Defence of History* (London: Granta, 1997), 7–8. .

59. Lipstadt, *History on Trial*, dedication page.

60. That position would seem to be at odds with Evans's claim that the trial "had nothing to do with any moral issues or lessons of any sort for future generations." Evans, *Lying About Hitler*, 259.

61. Henri Rousso, *The Haunting Past: History, Memory, and Justice in Contemporary France*, translated by Ralph Schoolcraft (Philadelphia: University of Pennsylvania Press, 2002), 22, 49 86. See also the summary provided by Richard Evans in "History, Memory, and the Law," 334–335, 338.

62. Douglas, *The Memory of Judgment*, 150ff., 260 (quotation).

63. Lipstadt, *History on Trial*, 25; Deborah E. Lipstadt, *Denying the Holocaust: The Growing Assault on Truth and Memory* (New York: Penguin, 1993), 213–214, 218. Lipstadt affirmed the importance of memory fortification in a series of email exchanges with me, 21–23 December 2015.

Conclusion

1. David Rieff, *In Praise of Forgetting: Historical Memory and Its Ironies* (New Haven: Yale University Press, 2016), 120. Rieff's interesting essay both draws on and converses with Yerushalmi's *Zakhor*, though in an important way misapprehends it. While there is a dolorous tone over the corrosive force of modernity in the last chapter of that book, Rieff goes too far in suggesting that Yerushalmi yearned for "some form of commanding authority" such as Halakah in the modern age or that he possessed a nostalgic "veneration of memory as the guarantor of tradition" (142). At least in *Zakhor*, Yerushalmi was too much the historian, indeed, too alive to dynamic change in history, to allow this. As he states in the Prologue, "the reader will not have understood me if he interprets the doubts and misgivings I express as meaning that I propose a return to prior modes of thought." Yosef Hayim Yerushalmi, *Zakhor: Jewish History and Jewish Memory*, rev. ed. (New York: Schocken, 1989), xxxvi. That said, I have suggested in the introduction that Yerushalmi elsewhere hinted at a more constructive role for history and the historian in fostering memory.

2. Michael R. Marrus, *Lessons of the Holocaust* (Toronto: University of Toronto Press, 2015), 7, 11.

3. Timothy D. Snyder, *Black Earth: The Holocaust as History and Warning* (New York: Tim Duggan Books, 2015), 343.

4. Ibid., 340.

5. Yerushalmi, *Zakhor*, 101.

6. Ibid., 100.

7. That question brings us back for a moment to the insights of brain

research, especially as advanced by the University of Southern California neuroscientist Antonio Damasio. Damasio has written of the brain's regulatory mechanisms, genetically refined and transmitted, that produce homeostasis, the state of equilibrium that allows us to function in the midst of upheaval and change. He makes reference not to the chemically induced homeostasis of the brain but rather to the sociocultural homeostasis of the group. "With culture," he observes, "we begin to regulate not only the life of the individual but the life of the individual within the social group." Susan Andrews, "Antonio Damasio Probes the Mind in His New Book," Medical Xpress, 12 November 2010, https://medical xpress.com/news/2010-11-antonio-damasio-probes-mind.html (accessed on 15 March 2017).

8. Yehuda Elkana, "The Need to Forget," *Haaretz*, 2 March 1988.

9. See, for example, the former Israeli politician Avraham Burg's *The Holocaust Is Over: We Must Rise from Its Ashes* (New York: Palgrave Macmillan, 2008), and the French historian Esther Benbassa's *Suffering as Identity: The Jewish Paradigm*, translated by G. M. Goshgarian (London: Verso, 2010).

10. On the role of the Shoah in Israeli public and political life, see inter alia Tom Segev, *The Seventh Million: The Israelis and the Holocaust*, translated by Haim Watzman (New York: Hill and Wang, 1993); Idith Zertal, *Israel's Holocaust and the Politics of Nationhood*, translated by Chaya Galai (Cambridge: Cambridge University Press, 2005); and Moshe Zuckerman, *Sho'ah ba-ḥeder ha-aṭum: ha-"Sho'ah" ba-'itonut ha-Yisre'elit bi-teḳufat Milḥemet ha-Mifraṣ* (Tel Aviv: Moshe Zuckerman, 1993). See also Saul Friedlander, "The Shoah in Present Historical Consciousness," in his *Memory, History, and the Extermination of the Jews of Europe* (Bloomington: Indiana University Press, 1993), 43–47, as well as Saul Friedlander and Adam Seligman, "The Israeli Memory of the Shoah: On Symbols, Rituals, and Ideological Polarization," in Roger Friedland and Deirdre Boden, eds. *NowHere: Space, Time and Modernity* (Berkeley: University of California Press, 1994), 356–371. See also Friedlander's lecture "Some Reflections on Transmitting the Memory of the Shoa," delivered at the Van Leer Institute, Jerusalem, on 10 October 2013, at https://www.youtube.com/watch?v=gfu2lJqWKOk. David Rieff also weighs in by declaring that "Israel offers a florid illustration of how disastrously collective memory can deform a society." *In Praise of Forgetting*, 139. For a wide-angle lens on the culture of "victimhood" in Israeli society, linking it to a global postmodern sensibility, see Alon Gan, *Korbanutam—umanutam: mi-siaḥ korbani le-siaḥ riboni* (Jerusalem: Israel Democracy Institute, 2014), available at

https://en.idi.org.il/media/3985/victimhood_book.pdf. I thank Dr. Nadav Molchadsky for calling my attention to this book.

11. Arlene Stein, "Too Much Memory? Holocaust Fatigue in the Era of the Victim," in Stein, *Reluctant Witnesses: Survivors, Their Children, and the Rise of Holocaust Consciousness* (Oxford: Oxford University Press, 2014), 166–182. See her opinion piece, "Holocaust Survivors Don't Belong in the Israeli-Palestinian Debate," *Haaretz*, 21 September 2014, available at http://www.haaretz.com/opinion/.premium-1.617059.

12. The controversy surrounding the German novelist Martin Walser's speech in 1998 about the "instrumentalizion" of the Holocaust sparked intense debate. See Kathrin Schödel, "Normalising Cultural Memory? The 'Walser-Bubis Debate' and Martin Walser's Novel *Ein springender Brunnen*," in Stuart Taberner and Frank Finlay, eds. *Recasting German Identity: Culture, Politics, and Literature in the Berlin Republic* (Rochester, N.Y.: Camden Hill, 2002), 67–84. An especially sharp formulation of the question of whether Holocaust memory is overprivileged in America came from the Yeshiva University student Binyamin Weinreich in his "Why It's Time for Jews to Get over the Holocaust," *The Beacon*, 21 February 2012, available at https://groups.google.com/forum/#!topic/davidshasha/is8WSLRMF2U.

13. Friedrich Nietzsche, *On the Advantage and Disadvantage of History for Life*, translated by Peter Preuss (Indianapolis: Hackett, 1980), 10, 14.

14. Richard England, "Coming to Terms with the Past: Northern Ireland," *History Today* 54 (July 2004), available at http://www.history today.com/richard-english/coming-terms-past-northern-ireland; Cillian McGrattan, "Historians in Post-Conflict Societies: Northern Ireland After the Troubles," *History and Policy*, 3 March 2011, http://www.history andpolicy.org/policy-papers/papers/historians-in-post-conflict-societies -northern-ireland-after-the-troubles. .

15. "IHJR Project on the Former Yugoslavia," Institute for Historical Justice and Reconciliation, http://historyandreconciliation.org/our-work/ projects/former-yugoslavia/ (accessed on 23 January 2017).

16. The goal of the Institute's work in the former Yugoslavia is to counter "some of the xenophobic national myths" and "bring attention to the similarities and overlapping experiences and identities among societies in the region in cultural, religion, social and political life." "IHJR Project on the Former Yugoslavia." .

17. See Motti Golani and Adel Manna, "Two Sides of the Coin: Independence and Nakba, 1948," Institute for Historical Justice and Reconciliation, http://historyandreconciliation.org/detailed-summary-two-sides

-of-the-coin-independence-and-nakba-1948/ (accessed on 23 January 2017). The Institute also sponsors research on the important role that historical memory plays in shaping present-day perceptions of the conflict. One study compares the reactions of Palestinian and Israeli university students to photographs of Palestinian refugees in 1948. Another explores the divergent historical memories of the city of Haifa, which is heralded by Jews as a unique space of harmony and peaceful coexistence and by Arabs as a once vibrant urban center undone by the Nakba. A third looks at the way in which the two groups relate to three holy sites. The common thread in these projects is "to encourage tolerance and understanding by familiarizing both sides with the narrative of the Other." For an overview of the Institute's projects on Israel and Palestine, see "IHJR Projects in Israel and the Palestinian Territories," Institute for Historical Justice and Reconciliation, http://historyandreconciliation.org/our-work/projects/israel-palestine/ (accessed on 20 September 2016).

18. The United States Institute for Peace supported a number of these initiatives, which are summarized in Richard H. Solomon, "Teaching Peace or War," United States Institute for Peace, http://www.usip.org/publications/teaching-peace-or-war (accessed on 23 January 2017). "Learning Each Other's Historical Narrative: Palestinians and Israelis," PRIME website, http://www.vispo.com/PRIME/leohn1.pdf (English translation of the Hebrew and Arabic text, accessed on 23 January 2017).

19. Viet Thanh Nguyen, *Nothing Ever Dies: Vietnam and the Memory of War* (Cambridge: Harvard University Press, 2016), 9.

20. In this regard, I take a very different stance from that of Aaron Hughes in his polemic against what he sees as an excess of identity politics in Jewish studies. See Hughes, *The Study of Judaism: Authenticity, Identity, Scholarship* (Albany: State University of New York Press, 2013). Hughes identifies with the subject of his biography, the extraordinarily prolific scholar Jacob Neusner, who criticized scholars in the field of Jewish studies as overly beholden to the uncritical traditionalism of the "yeshiva," as distinct from his own fealty to the critical methodology of the "university." See Aaron W. Hughes, *Jacob Neusner: An American Jewish Iconoclast* (New York: New York University, 2016), 4ff. In an unpublished paper, "On Identity and Scholarly Engagement," delivered at the 2016 summer institute of the Oxford Centre for Hebrew and Jewish Studies, I argued, contra Hughes (and, by extension, Neusner), in defense of the scholar's identitarian investment in the object of his or her research.

21. In telling fashion, even such a vocal and long-standing advocate of the two-state ideal as the *New York Times* columnist Thomas Friedman

now casts doubt on its prospects. See Friedman, "The Many Mideast Solutions," *New York Times*, 10 February 2016, available at http://www.ny times.com/2016/02/10/opinion/the-many-mideast-solutions.html?_r=0.

22. Benny Morris, *One State, Two States: Resolving the Israel/Palestine Conflict* (New Haven: Yale University Press, 2009), 34–55.

23. On Ben-Gurion's proposal to Alami, see Morris, *One State, Two States*, 197. See also the proposed constitution formulated by a group under the banner Israel-Palestine Confederation at http://www.ipconfederation .org/constitution-english.htm, as well as Uri Avnery's "An Israeli-Palestinian Federation Is Still the Way," *Haaretz* 8 August 2013, available at http:// www.haaretz.com/opinion/1.540551. On the canton system see Morris, *One State, Two States,* 59, Meron Benvenisti, "Which Kind of Binational State?" *Haaretz*, 20 November 2003, available at http://odspi.org/articles/ benvenisti.html, and Carlo Strenger, "Divide Israel into Cantons," *Haaretz*, 29 March 2014, available at http://www.haaretz.com/opinion/.premium -1.582591. On two-state schemes, in addition to Morris's discussion in *One State, Two State,* see the recent proposal for a two-state scheme in which the two states do not possess their own discrete territories but rather inhabit jointly the terrain between the river and the sea in Mark LeVine and Mathias Mossberg, eds. *One Land, Two States: Israel and Palestine as Parallel States* (Berkeley: University of California Press, 2014).

24. See, for example, the proposal by Israel's Permanent Representative to the United Nations, Danny Danon, "The Three State Solution," *Foreign Policy*, 2 June 2014, http://foreignpolicy.com/2014/06/02/the-three -state-solution-2/.

25. After casting doubt on the prospects for one- and two-state options, Morris briefly considers a combined West Bank-Gaza-Jordan state as the best option available, even if unlikely. Morris, *One State, Two States,* 193–201.

26. This impulse resonates with the spirit of "sideshadowing," reconsidering forgotten moments from the path that did not conform to our received teleological narrative, that Michael André Bernstein discusses in *Foregone Conclusions: Against Apocalyptic History* (Berkeley: University of California Press, 1994), esp. chap. 5.

27. Even if we cannot realize the promise of grasping history "as it actually was," Wyschogrod argues, we must do all within our power to discharge the obligation to "give countenance," especially in an age of mass murder when there are so many victims whose names, voices, and faces are lost. Edith Wyschogrod, *An Ethics of Remembering: History, Heterology, and the Nameless Others* (Chicago: University of Chicago Press, 1998), xii.

28. Some of the problems that Henri Rousso raised in objecting to historians as witnesses have also figured in the work of history writing in truth and reconciliation processes. In discussing the somewhat strained relationship between historians and the truth and reconciliation process in South Africa, Jacobus Du Pisani and Kwang-Su Kim observe: "Historians are committed to the never ending debate of history and not to the type of closure sought by priests and politicians." Du Pisani and Kim, "Establishing the Truth About the Apartheid Past: Historians and the South African Truth and Reconciliation Commission," *African Studies Quarterly* 8 (Fall 2004): 77–95. Elazar Barkan, a leading figure in bringing historians to the work of reconciliation, convened a roundtable, "Truth and Reconciliation in History," to discuss the potentially therapeutic labors of historians in reconciling Jews and Poles, Turks and Armenians, and the peoples of the former Yugoslavia. See Barkan, "Historians and Historical Reconciliation," *American Historical Review* 114 (2009): 899–913.

29. In discussing this "alternate ethics, Viet Thanh Nguyen writes: "If the ethics of remembering one's own operates in every society, the ethics of remembering others is the refinement of remembering one's own." He goes on to warn of the dangers of a society using its ethics of remembering as a cover to attack a group it believes does not match its ethical standards. Nguyen, *Nothing Ever Dies*, 9–11, 47–70 (quotation at 69).

30. The link is evident in the title of the report: "The Report of the Working Group on Slavery, Memory, and Reconciliation to the President of Georgetown University," Summer 2016, available at http://slavery .georgetown.edu/ (accessed on 30 September 2016), 33. In the wake of this report, Harvard University president Drew Gilpin Faust, convened a scholarly conference in March 2016 to examine the relationship between American universities and their former slave holdings. At the conference, the author Ta-Nehisi Coates renewed his call from 2014 for reparations to be given to descendants of slaves as an act of restorative justice. See Jennifer Schuessler, "Confronting Academia's Slavery Ties," *New York Times*, 6 March 2017, as well as Ta-Nehisi Coates, "The Case for Reparations," *The Atlantic* (June 2014), available at https://www.theatlantic.com/magazine/ archive/2014/06/the-case-for-reparations/361631/.

31. Richard Neustadt and Ernest R. May, *Thinking in Time: The Uses of History for Decision Makers* (New York: Free Press, 1986), xi, 32–33.

32. Graham Allison and Niall Ferguson, "Why the U.S. President Needs a Council of Historians," The Atlantic Online, September 2016, http://www.theatlantic.com/magazine/archive/2016/09/dont-know-much -about-history/492746/.

33. Jo Guldi and David Armitage, *The History Manifesto* (Cambridge: Cambridge University Press, 2014), 13–19. For a critique of their view that history has succumbed to "short-termism," see above, Introduction, n. 8.

34. Hobsbawm reflected on the predictive capacity of historians in a 1981 lecture, "Looking Forward: History and the Future," reprinted in Hobsbawm, *On History* (New York: New Press, 1997), 38.

35. Two important institutional manifestations of that willingness are the creation of the Lepage Center for History in the Public Interest at Villanova University and the Luskin Center for History and Policy at UCLA in 2017.

36. There is a wide literature on the debates among Israeli historians, including those who began, from the late 1980s, to challenge foundational myths of Israel history. For a range of views, see Yechiam Weitz, ed. *Ben hazon le-revizyah: me'ah shenot historiyografyah Tsionit* (Jerusalem: Zalman Shazar Center, 1997), Laurence J. Silberstein, *The Postzionism Debates: Knowledge and Power in Israeli Culture* (New York: Routledge, 1999), and Yoav Gelber, *Nation and History: Israeli Historiography Between Zionism and Post-Zionism* (Middlesex, UK: Vallentine Mitchell, 2011). The so-called New Historians included Benny Morris, who laid out his cohort's brief in "The New Historiography: Israel Confronts Its Past," *Tikkun* 3 (1988): 19–23, 98–103. Morris was challenged shortly thereafter by the veteran historian and journalist Shabtai Tevet in "Charging Israel with Original Sin," *Commentary* (September 1989): 24–33, and, a decade later, by the renowned historian Anita Shapira, "The Past Is Not a Foreign Country: The Failure of Israel's 'New Historians' to Explain War and Peace," *New Republic*, 29 November 1999, 26–36. In the meantime, Morris had parted ways with fellow New Historians, as reflected in a provocative interview with Ari Shavit in *Haaretz* on 9 January 2004, available at http://www.haaretz.com/survival-of-the-fittest-1.61345 (accessed on 5 February 2017), and later in a review of his contemporary Ilan Pappé in Morris, "The Liar as Hero," *New Republic*, 16 March 2011, 29–35.

37. Yerushalmi, "Postscript: Reflections on Forgetting," *Zakhor*, 116–117.

38. Ibid., 117. See also Rieff, *In Defense of Forgetting*, 99.

39. This proverb in the Ewe-Mina language is found in Jennifer Speake, ed., *The Oxford Dictionary of Proverbs*, 6th ed. (Oxford: Oxford University Press, 2015), 185.

Postscript

1. See Samuel Moyn, "Bonfire of the Humanities," *Nation*, 21 January 2015, available at http://www.thenation.com/article/195553/bonfire-humanities.

2. Baron saw *The Contemporary Relevance of History* as a methodological "appendix" to his massive *Social and Religious History of the Jews*. He lamented that "most Jewish historians did not bother to come to grips with the basic philosophical and methodological aspects of their craft, but merely devoted their energies to describing historical events and movements in some narrative or analytical fashion appealing to them." Salo W. Baron, *The Contemporary Relevance of History* (New York: Columbia University Press, 1986), vii, 41. Meanwhile, Moshe Rosman set out to grapple with the challenges of writing history in a postmodern age replete with skepticism toward the very idea of historical truth. His own attempts to navigate between the poles of "essentialism" and "constructivism" lead him to a middle ground in which the historian can grasp a wide range of "historical experiences and historical perspectives" without succumbing to "the most extreme postmodern epistemological and methodological strictures." Rosman, *How Jewish Is Jewish History?* (Oxford: Littman Library of Jewish Civilization, 2007), 186.

3. Leopold von Ranke, *Englische Geschichte vornehmlich im siebzehnten Jahurhundert* (Leipzig: Duncker und Humblot, 1877), 103.

4. Roland Barthes, "The Discourse of History," translated by Stephen Bann, *Comparative Criticism* 3 (1981): 7. See also Hayden White, "The Question of Narrative in Contemporary Historical Theory," *History and Theory* 23 (February 1984): 1–33.

5. White, "The Question of Narrative in Contemporary Historical Theory," 5.

6. For a helpful distinction between naive historical realism based on immediate perception and a more deliberate and reasoned form of historical realism, see C. Bevan McCullogh, "Historical Realism," *Philosophy and Phenomenological Research*. 40, no. 3 (March, 1980):420–425. White has a rather unconventional view of "realism," holding that "'the true' is identified with 'the real' only insofar as it can be shown to possess the character of narrativity." Hayden White, *The Content of the Form: Narrative Discourse and Historical Representation* (Baltimore: Johns Hopkins University Press, 1987), 6.

7. The intellectual historian John E. Toews notes some of the limits of this approach in his important article "Intellectual History After the Linguistic Turn: The Autonomy of Meaning and the Irreducibility of Experience," *American Historical Review* 92 (1987): esp. 882.

8. See the volume edited by the conference organizer, Saul Friedlander, *Probing the Limits of Representation: Nazism and the "Final Solution"* (Cambridge: Harvard University Press, 1992).

9. Quoted in White, "The Question of Narrative in Contemporary Historical Theory," 3.

10. This view found enthusiastic adherents in the 1930s in the United States in the work of distinguished scholars such as Charles Beard and Carl Becker, the latter of whom echoed Croce in his presidential address to the American Historical Association in December 1931, "Everyman His Own Historian." After recalling Croce and the idea that all history is contemporary, Becker declared that "in so far as we think the past . . . it becomes an integral and living part of our present world of semblance." Carl Becker, "Everyman His Own Historian," in Becker, *Everyman His Own Historian: Essays on History and Politics* (New York: F. S. Crofts, 1935), 242.

11. R. G. Collingwood, *The Idea of History*, edited by Jan Van Der Dussen (Oxford: Oxford University Press, 1993), 282–283.

12. Ibid., 291–292.

13. As Collingwood puts it in his "Lectures on the Philosophy of History" (1926): "It may seem paradoxical to say that one account is nearer to the truth than another while yet confessing that we do not know what the truth is; but we must face this paradox." Collingwood, *The Idea of History*, 391. It is important to add that Collingwood himself, in contrast to the perspective advanced in this book, distinguished sharply between the function and nature of history and memory. Ibid., 252–253. See as well as the comparison of Dilthey and Collingwood in Geoffrey Cubitt, *History and Memory* (Manchester: Manchester University Press, 2007), 32–35.

BIBLIOGRAPHY

Adams, Hannah. *History of the Jews from the Destruction of Jerusalem to the Present Time.* 2 vols. Boston: J. Eliot, Jr., 1812.

Amstutz, H., et al., eds. *Fuzzy Boundaries: Festschrift für Antonio Loprieno.* Hamburg: Widmaier Verlag, 2015.

Appleby, Joyce, Lynn Hunt, and Margaret Jacob. *Telling the Truth About History.* New York: Norton, 1994.

Aran, Gideon, and Ron E. Hassner. "Religious Violence in Judaism: Past and Present." *Terrorism and Political Violence* 25, no. 3 (2013): 355–405.

Arendt, Hannah. *Eichmann in Jerusalem: A Report on the Banality of Evil.* New York. Viking, 1963.

Armitage, David, and Jo Guldi. *The History Manifesto.* Cambridge: Cambridge University Press, 2014.

Assman, Jan. *Moses the Egyptian: The Memory of Egypt in Western Monotheism.* Cambridge: Harvard University Press, 1997.

Baer, Yitzhak. *Galut.* Translated by Robert Warshow. New York: Schocken, 1947.

———. *Yisra'el ba-'amim.* Jerusalem: Mosad Bialik, 1955.

Baldwin, Peter. *Hitler, the Holocaust and the Historians Dispute.* Boston: Beacon, 1990.

Bambach, Charles R. *Heidegger, Dilthey, and the Crisis of Historicism.* Ithaca: Cornell University Press, 1995.

Bankier, David, and Dan Michman, eds. *Holocaust Historiography in Context: Emergence, Challenges, Polemics and Achievements.* Jerusalem: Yad Vashem, 2008.

Baron, Salo W. *The Contemporary Relevance of History.* New York: Columbia University Press, 1986.

———. "Ghetto and Emancipation: Shall We Revise the Traditional View?" *Menorah Journal* 14 (June 1928): 515–526.

———. "The Revolution of 1848 and Jewish Scholarship: Part 1: France, the United States and Italy." *Proceedings of the American Academy for Jewish Research* 18 (1948–1949): 1–66.

———. "The Revolution of 1848 and Jewish Scholarship: Part 2: Austria." *Proceedings of the American Academy for Jewish Research* 20 (1951): 1–100.

———. *A Social and Religious History of the Jews*. Vol. 2. New York: Columbia University Press, 1937.

Baskin, Judith R., ed. *Jewish Women in Historical Perspective*. Detroit: Wayne State University Press, 1991.

Basnage, Jacques. *The History of the Jews, from Jesus Christ to the Present Time: Containing Their Antiquities, Their Religion, Their Rites, the Dispersion of the Ten Tribes in the East and the Persecutions This Nation Has Suffer'd in the West. Being a Supplement and Continuation of the History of Josephus*. London: J. Beaver and B. Lintot, 1708.

Bauer, Yehuda. *Rethinking the Holocaust*. New Haven: Yale University Press, 2002.

Becker, Carl L. *Everyman His Own Historian: Essays on History and Politics*. New York: F. S. Crofts, 1935.

Beer, Peter. *Geschichte, Lehren und Meinungen aller bestandenen und noch bestehenden religiösen Sekten der Juden und der Geheimlehre oder Kabbalah*. 2 vols. Brünn: J. G. Trassler, 1822, 1823.

———. *Toldot Yisra'el*. Vienna: Anton Edlen von Schmid, 1833.

Beiser, Frederick. *The German Historicist Tradition*. Oxford: Oxford University Press, 2011.

Benbassa, Esther. *Suffering as Identity: The Jewish Paradigm*. Translated by G. M. Goshgarian. London: Verso, 2010.

Bernfeld, Shimon. *Sefer ha-dema'ot: me'ora'ot ha-gezerot veha-redifot veha-shemadot*. 3 vols. Berlin: Hotsa'ot Eshkol, 1923–1926.

Bérubé, Michael. "The Humanities Declining? Not According to the Numbers." *Chronicle of Higher Education* 1 July 2013. http://www.chronicle.com/article/The-Humanities-Declining-Not/140093/.

Bloch, Marc. *The Historian's Craft*. Translated by Peter Putnam. New York: Vintage, 1953.

Bloxham, Donald. *Genocide on Trial: War Crimes Trials and the Formation of Holocaust History and Memory*. Oxford: Oxford University Press, 2001.

Blumenberg, Hans. *The Legitimacy of the Modern Age*. Cambridge: MIT Press, 1985.

Boden, Deirdre, and Roger Friedland eds. *NowHere: Space, Time and Modernity*. Berkeley: University of California Press, 1994.

Brenner, Michael. *Prophets of the Past: Interpreters of Jewish History*. Translated by Steven Rendall. Princeton: Princeton University Press, 2010.

———. *A Short History of the Jews*. Translated by Jeremiah Riemer. Princeton: Princeton University Press, 2010.

Brenner, Michael, and David N. Myers, eds. *Jüdische Geschichtsschreibung heute: Themen, Positionen, Kontroversen*. Munich: Beck Verlag, 2002.

Brinkman, Tobias. "Memory and Modern Jewish History in Contemporary Germany." *Shofar* 4 (1997): 17–18.

Brot, Rivka. "Ben kehilah li-medinah: mishpatehem shel meshatfe pe'ulah Yehudim 'im Natsim." Ph.D. diss., Tel Aviv University, 2015.

Burckhardt, Jacob. *On History and Historians.* Translated by Harry Zohn. New York: Harper and Row, 1958.

Burg, Avraham. *The Holocaust Is Over: We Must Rise from Its Ashes.* New York: Palgrave Macmillan, 2008.

Buruma, Ian. *The Wages of Guilt: Memories of War in Germany and Japan.* New York: Farrar, Straus and Giroux, 1994.

Butterfield, Herbert. *The Englishman and His History.* Hamden, Conn.: Archon, 1970.

Carlebach, Elisheva. "Between History and Hope: Jewish Messianism in Ashkenaz and Sepharad." Third Annual Lecture of the Victor Selmanowitz Chair of Jewish History, Touro College, New York, 1998.

Carlebach, Elisheva, John M. Efron, and David N. Myers, eds., *Jewish History and Jewish Memory: Essays in Honor of Yosef Hayim Yerushalmi.* Hanover, N.H.: Brandeis University Press, 1998.

Carr, E. H. *What Is History?* New York: Penguin, 1961.

Chatterjee, Partha, and Anjan Ghosh, eds. *History and the Present.* Delhi: Permanent Black, 2002.

Chazan, Robert. *God, Humanity, and History: The Hebrew First Crusade Narratives.* Berkeley: University of California Press, 2000.

Cohen, Boaz. *Holocaust and Justice: Representation and Historiography of the Holocaust in Post-War Trials.* Jerusalem: Yad Vashem and Berghahn, 2011.

Cohen, Deborah, and Peter Mandler. "The History Manifesto: A Critique." *American Historical Review* 120, no. 2 (2015): 530–542.

Cohen, Gerson D. *The Book of Tradition (Sefer Ha-Qabbalah) by Abraham ibn Daud.* Philadelphia: Jewish Publication Society, 1967.

Cohen, Jeremy. *Sanctifying the Name of God: Jewish Martyrs and Jewish Memories of the First Crusade.* Philadelphia: University of Pennsylvania Press, 2006.

Collingwood, R. G. *The Idea of History.* Edited by Jan Van Der Dussen. Oxford: Oxford University Press, 1993.

Confino, Alon. "Collective Memory and Cultural History: Problems of Method." *American Historical Review* 102, no. 5 (1997): 1386–1403.

Conot, Robert. *Justice at Nuremberg.* New York: Harper and Row, 1983.

Cover, Robert M. "Folktales of Justice: Tales of Jurisdiction." *Capital University Law Review* 14, no. 179 (1984–1985): 189–190.

———. "Nomos and Narrative." *Harvard Law Review* 97, no. 4 (1983–1984): 4–68.

Coy, Jason, et al., eds. *Kinship, Community, and Self: Essays in Honor of David Warren Sabean.* New York: Berghahn, 2014.

Croce, Benedetto. *History as the Story of Liberty.* Translated by Sylvia Sprigge. Chicago: Henry Regnery, 1941.

Dinur (Dinaburg), Ben Zion. *Yisra'el ba-Golah.* Tel Aviv: Devir and Mosad Bialik, 1958.

Dosse, François. *Pierre Nora: Homo Historicus.* Paris: Perrin, 2011.

Douglas, Lawrence. *The Memory of Judgment: Making Law and History in the Trials of the Holocaust.* New Haven: Yale University Press, 2001.

Duberman, Martin. *Howard Zinn: Life on the Left.* New York: New Press, 2012.

Dubnov-Erlich, Sophie. *The Life and Work of S. J. Dubnow.* Bloomington: Indiana University Press, 1991.

Dubnow, Simon. Introduction to *Anṭisemiṭism un pogromen in Ukraine, 1917–1918: tsu der geshikhṭe fun Ukrainish-Yidishe batsihungen.* Berlin: Mizreḥ-Yidishn hisṭorishn arkhiv, 1923.

———. *Nationalism and History: Essays on Old and New Judaism.* Edited by Koppel S. Pinson. Philadelphia: Jewish Publication Society, 1958.

———. "Sod ha-kiyum ve-hok ha-kiyum shel 'am Yisra'el" (The Secret of Survival—and the Law of Survival—of the Jewish People). *He-'atid* 7 (1923): 112–117.

Ehrenberg, Ilya, and Vasily Grossman. *The Complete Black Book of Russian Jewry.* Translated and edited by David Patterson. New Brunswick, N.J.: Transaction, 2009.

Ehrenfreund, Jacques. *Les Juifs berlinois à la Belle Époque.* Paris: Presses Universitaires de France, 2000.

Eidelberg, Shlomo, ed. *The Jews and the Crusaders: The Hebrew Chronicles of the First and Second Crusades.* Madison: University of Wisconsin Press, 1977.

Elon, Amos. *The Pity of It All: A Portrait of the German-Jewish Epoch, 1743–1933.* New York: Metropolitan Books, 2002.

Ellenson, David. *Rabbi Esriel Hildesheimer and the Creation of a Modern Jewish Orthodoxy.* Tuscaloosa: University of Alabama Press, 1990.

Ellenson, David, and Richard Jacobs. "Scholarship and Faith: David Hoffmann and His Relation to Wissenschaft des Judentums." *Modern Judaism* 8 (1988): 27–40.

Elukin, Jonathan M. "Jacques Basnage and the History of the Jews: Anti-Catholic Polemic and Historical Allegory in the Republic of Letters." *Journal of the History of Ideas* 53, no. 4 (October–December 1992): 603–630.

Engel, David. "Being Lawful in a Lawless World: The Trial of Scholem Schwarzbard and the Defense of East European Jews." *Simon Dubnow Institute Yearbook* 5 (2006): 83–97.

————. *Historians of the Jews and the Holocaust.* Stanford, Calif.: Stanford University Press, 2010.

Erik-Rose, Sven. *Jewish Philosophical Politics in Germany, 1789–1848.* Waltham, Mass.: Brandeis University Press, 2014.

Evans, Richard J. "History, Memory and the Law: The Historian as Expert Witness." *History and Theory* 41 (2002): 326–345.

————. *In Defence of History.* London: Granta, 1997.

————. *In Hitler's Shadow: West German Historians and the Attempt to Escape the Nazi Past.* New York: Pantheon, 1989.

————. *Lying About Hitler: History, Holocaust, and the David Irving Trial.* New York: Basic, 2001.

Evers, Renate. "Die 'Schocken-Bücherei' in den Nachlasssammlungen des Leo Baeck Institutes New York." *Medaon* 14 (2014). http://www.medaon .de/de/artikel/die-schocken-buecherei-in-den-nachlasssammlungen -des-leo-baeck-institutes-new-york/.

Finder, Gabriel, and Laura Jockusch. *Jewish Honor Courts: Revenge, Retribution, and Reconciliation in Europe and Israel After the Holocaust.* Detroit: Wayne State University Press, 2015.

Fink, Carole. *Marc Bloch: A Life in History.* Cambridge: Cambridge University Press, 1989.

Fram, Yehezkel (Edward). "Ben TaTNaV (1096) le-TaH/TaT (1648–49): 'iyun mi-hadash." *Zion* 61 (1996): 159–182.

Frank, Daniel H., and Oliver Leaman eds. *History of Jewish Philosophy.* London: Routledge, 1997.

Friedlander, Saul. *Memory, History, and the Extermination of the Jews of Europe.* Bloomington: Indiana University Press, 1993.

Friedlander, Saul, ed. *Probing the Limits of Representation: Nazism and the "Final Solution."* Cambridge: Harvard University Press, 1992.

Friedman, Philip. *Roads to Extinction: Essays on the Holocaust.* New York: Jewish Publication Society of America, 1980.

Friedman, Saul S. *Pogromchick: The Assassination of Simon Petlura.* New York: Hart, 1976.

Funkenstein, Amos. *Perspectives on Jewish History.* Berkeley: University of California Press, 1993.

————. "Toldot Yisra'el ben ha-hohim: ha-historyah le-mul distsiplinot aherot." *Zion* 60 (1995): 335–347.

Fussell, Paul. *The Great War and Modern Memory.* New York: Oxford University Press, 1975.

Gardiner, Patrick, ed. *Theories of History.* Glencoe, Ill.: Free Press, 1959.

Gay, Peter, and Gerald J. Cavanaugh, eds. *Historians at Work.* Vol. 1. New York: Harper and Row, 1972.

Geary, Patrick J. *The Myth of Nations: The Medieval Origins of Europe.* Princeton: Princeton University Press, 2002.

Geiger, Abraham. *Abraham Geiger's Nachgelassene Schriften.* Vol. 1. Edited by Ludwig Geiger. Berlin: Louis Gerschel Verlagsbuchhandlung, 1875.

Gelber, Yoav. *Nation and History: Israeli Historiography Between Zionism and Post-Zionism.* Middlesex, U.K.: Vallentine Mitchell, 2011.

Gertner, Haim. "Reshitah shel ketivah historit ortodoksit be-Mizrah Eropah: Ha-ʿarakhah mehudeshet." *Zion* 67, no. 3 (2002): 293–336.

Ginzburg, Carlo. *The Judge and the Historian: Marginal Notes on a Late-Twentieth-Century Miscarriage of Justice.* Translated by Antony Shugaar. London: Verso, 1999.

Glatzer, Nahum N., ed. *Leopold and Adelheid Zunz: An Account in Letters, 1815–1885.* London: East and West Library, 1958.

———. *Leopold Zunz: Jude—Deutscher—Europaer.* Tübingen: Mohr, 1964.

Graetz, Heinrich. *History of the Jews.* Vol. 6. Philadelphia: Jewish Publication Society, 1898.

Halbwachs, Maurice. *The Collective Memory.* New York: Harper and Row, 1980.

———. *On Collective Memory.* Edited by Lewis Coser. Chicago: University of Chicago Press, 1992.

Harris, Jay M. *Nachman Krochmal: Guiding the Perplexed of the Modern Age.* New York: New York University Press, 1991.

Hartog, François. *Régimes d'historicité: présentisme et expérience du temps.* Paris: Éditions du Seuil, 2003.

Hartston, Barnet. *Sensationalizing the Jewish Question: Anti-Semitic Trials and the Press in the Early German Empire.* Leiden: Brill, 2015.

Harvey, Van Austin. *The Historians and the Believer.* New York: Macmillan, 1966.

Haverkamp, Eva. *Hebräische Berichte über die Judenverfolgungen während des Ersten Kreuzzugs* [Hebrew Accounts of the Persecutions of the Jews During the First Crusade]. Hannover: Hahnsche Buchhandlung, 2005.

Hecht, Louise. *Ein jüdischer Aufklärer in Böhmen: Der Pädagoge und Reformer Peter Beer (1758–1838).* Cologne: Böhlau, 2008.

Heschel, Susannah. *Abraham Geiger and the Jewish Jesus.* Chicago: University of Chicago Press, 1998.

Hobsbawm, E. J. *Nations and Nationalism Since 1780.* Cambridge: Cambridge University Press, 1990.

Howard, Thomas A. *Religion and the Rise of Historicism: W. M. L. de Wette, Jacob Burckhardt and the Theological Origins of Nineteenth-Century Historical Consciousness.* Cambridge: Cambridge University Press, 2000.

Hughes, Aaron W. *Jacob Neusner: An American Jewish Iconoclast.* New York: New York University, 2016.

————. *The Study of Judaism: Authenticity, Identity, Scholarship*. Albany: State University of New York Press, 2013.

Hughes, Stuart H. *History as Art and as Science*. New York: Harper and Row, 1964.

Hunt, Lynn. *Writing History in the Global Era*. New York: Norton, 2014.

Hyman, Paula E. *Gender and Assimilation in Modern Jewish History*. Seattle: University of Washington Press, 1995.

————. "Immigrant Women and Consumer Protest: The New York City Kosher Meat Boycott of 1902." *American Jewish History* 70, no. 1 (1980): 91–105.

————. *Jewish Feminism Faces the American Women's Movement: Convergence and Divergence*. Ann Arbor, Mich.: Jean and Samuel Frankel Center for Judaic Studies, 1997.

Jawitz, Zeev. *Sefer Toldot Yisra'el*. 3rd ed. Berlin: Yerah Etanim, 1924–1925.

Jellison, Katherine. "History in the Courtroom: The Sears Case in Perspective." *Public Historian* 9 (1987): 9–19.

Jenkins, Keith. *On "What Is History?"* London: Routledge, 1995.

Jockusch, Laura. *Collect and Record! Jewish Holocaust Documentation in Early Postwar Europe*. New York: Oxford University Press, 2015.

————. "Introductory Remarks on Simon Dubnow's 'Let Us Seek and Investigate.'" In *Simon-Dubnow-Institut Jahrbuch*, 7: 343–382. Leipzig: Vandenhoeck and Ruprecht, 2008.

Johnson, Kelly Scott. "Scholem Schwarzbard: Biography of a Jewish Assassin." Ph.D. diss., Harvard University, 2012.

Kalmar, Ivan, and Derek Penslar, eds. *Orientalism and the Jews*. Waltham, Mass.: Brandeis University Press, 2005.

Karlinsky, Nahum. *Historyah sheke-neged: "Igrot ha-ḥasidim me-Eretz-Yisra'el."* Ha-tekst veha-kontekst. Jerusalem: Yad Ben-Zvi, 1998.

Karlip, Joshua M. *The Tragedy of a Generation*. Cambridge: Harvard University Press, 2013.

Kassow, Samuel D. *Who Will Write Our History? Emanuel Ringelblum and the Oyneg Shabes Archive*. Bloomington: Indiana University Press, 2007.

Katz, David S., and Jonathan Israel, eds. *Sceptics, Millenarians, and Jews*. Leiden: Brill, 1990.

Klausner, Yosef. "Megamatenu." *Ha-Shiloah* 11 (1903): 1–10.

Klein, Birgit. "Warum studieren in Deutschland Nichtjüdinnen und Nichtjuden Judaistik?" *Judaica* 49 (1993): 33–41.

Klugman, Eliyahu Meir. *Rabbi Samson Raphael Hirsch*. Brooklyn, N.Y.: Mesorah Publications, 1996.

Koch, Leo. "Professor Shimon Dubnow un zayn barbarishe talmid." *Yidishe Kultur* 7 (1945): 39.

Kressel, G. "Shalom Baron 'im 'eduto be-mishpat Eichmann." *Davar* 25 (1961): 2.

Kreutzberger, M., ed. *Studies of the Leo Baeck Institute*. New York: Unger, 1967.

Krieger, Leonard. *Ranke: The Meaning of History*. Chicago: University of Chicago Press, 1977.

Kuznitz, Cecile Esther. *YIVO and the Making of Modern Jewish Culture: Scholarship for the Yiddish Nation*. Cambridge: Cambridge University Press, 2014.

Lang, Berel. *Philosophical Witnessing: The Holocaust as Presence*. Waltham, Mass.: Brandeis University Press, 2009.

Lerner, Gerda. *Living with History/Making Social Change*. Chapel Hill: University of North Carolina Press, 2009.

———. *Why History Matters: Life and Thought*. New York: Oxford University Press, 1997.

Levi, Primo. *The Reawakening*. Translated by Stuart Woolf. New York: Collier, 1987.

LeVine, Mark, and Mathias Mossberg, eds. *One Land, Two States: Israel and Palestine as Parallel States*. Berkeley: University of California Press, 2014.

Liberles, Robert. *Salo Wittmayer Baron: Architect of Jewish History*. New York: New York University Press, 1995.

Lipstadt, Deborah E. *Denying the Holocaust: The Growing Assault on Truth and Memory*. New York: Penguin, 1993.

———. *History on Trial: My Day in Court with David Irving*. New York: Ecco, 2005.

Löwith, Karl. *Meaning in History: The Theological Implications of the Philosophy of History*. Chicago: University of Chicago Press, 1949.

MacIntyre, Alasdair, and Paul Ricoeur. *The Religious Significance of Atheism*. New York: Columbia University Press, 1969.

MacMillan, Margaret. *Dangerous Games: The Uses and Abuses of History*. New York: Modern Library, 2008.

Makkreel, Rudolf A. *Dilthey: Philosopher of the Human Studies*. Princeton: Princeton University Press, 1975.

Marcus, Ivan. "From Politics to Martyrdom: Shifting Paradigms in the Hebrew Narratives of the 1096 Crusader Riots." *Prooftexts* 2 (1982): 40–52.

Marrus, Michael R. *Lessons of the Holocaust*. Toronto: University of Toronto Press, 2015.

———. *The Nuremberg War Crimes Trial, 1945–46*. Boston: Bedford, 1997.

McCullogh, C. Bevan. "Historical Realism." *Philosophy and Phenomenological Research* 40 (1980): 420–425.

Melamed, Hillel. "Vo azoy di nazis hobn dermordet Prof. Sh. Dubnow." *Di tsukunft* 51 (1946): 320–321.

Mendes-Flohr, Paul, and Jehuda Reinharz, eds. *The Jew in the Modern World: A Documentary History*. New York: Oxford University Press, 2011.

Meyer, Michael A. "Heinrich Graetz and Heinrich von Treitschke: A Comparison of Their Historical Images of the Modern Jew." *Modern Judaism* 6 (1986): 1–11.

——. *Ideas of Jewish History*. New York: Behrman House, 1974.

——. *The Origins of the Modern Jew*. Detroit: Wayne State University Press, 1967.

——. "Two Persistent Tensions Within *Wissenschaft des Judentums*." *Modern Judaism* 24 (2004): 105–119.

Meyer, Michael A., Michael Brenner, and Mordechai Breuer. *German-Jewish History in Modern Times: Emancipation and Acculturation*. New York: Columbia University Press, 1997

Michael, Reuven. *Ha-ketivah ha-historit ha-Yehudit*. Jerusalem: Mosad Bialik, 1993.

Milkman, Ruth. "Women's History and the Sears Case." *Feminist Studies* 12, no. 2 (1986): 375–400.

Miłosz, Czesław. *The Witness of Poetry*. Cambridge: Harvard University Press, 1983.

Mintz, Alan. *Hurban: Responses to Catastrophe in Hebrew Literature*. New York: Columbia University Press, 1984.

Molchadsky, Nadav G. "History in the Public Courtroom: Commissions of Inquiry and Struggles over the History and Memory of Israeli Traumas." Ph.D. diss., University of California, Los Angeles, 2015.

Morris, Benny. *One State, Two States: Resolving the Israel/Palestine Conflict*. New Haven: Yale University Press, 2009.

Myers, David N. "History and Memory in Jewish Studies: Overcoming the Chasm." In Mitchell B. Hart and Tony Michels, eds., *The Cambridge History of Judaism*, vol. 8: *The Modern World, 1815–2000*, 804–830. Cambridge: Cambridge University Press, 2017.

——. "'Mehabevin et ha-tarot': Crusade Memories and Modern Jewish Martyrologies." *Jewish History* 13, no. 2 (1999): 50–64.

——. *Re-Inventing the Jewish Past: European Jewish Intellectuals and the Zionist Return to History*. New York: Oxford University Press, 1995.

——. *Resisting History: Historicism and Its Discontents in German-Jewish Thought*. Princeton: Princeton University Press, 2003.

——. "The Scholem-Kurzweil Debate and Modern Jewish Historiography," *Modern Judaism* 6 (1986): 261–286.

Myers, David N., and Alexander Kaye, eds. *The Faith of Fallen Jews: Yosef Hayim Yerushalmi and the Writing of Jewish History*. Hanover, N.H.: Brandeis University Press, 2014.

Neustadt, Richard, and Ernest R. May. *Thinking in Time: The Uses of History for Decision Makers.* New York: Free Press, 1986.

Nguyen, Viet Thanh. *Nothing Ever Dies: Vietnam and the Memory of War.* Cambridge: Harvard University Press, 2016.

Nietzsche, Friedrich. *On the Advantage and Disadvantage of History for Life.* Translated by Peter Preuss. Indianapolis: Hackett, 1980.

Nirenberg, David. *Anti-Judaism: The Western Tradition.* New York: Norton, 2013.

Nora, Pierre. "Between Memory and History: *Les lieux de mémoire.*" *Representations* 26 (1989): 7–24.

———. *Realms of Memory: The Construction of the French Past.* Translated by Arthur Goldhammer. New York: Columbia University Press, 1996.

Paucker, Arnold, et al., eds. *Die Juden im Nationalsozialistischen Deutschland: The Jews in Nazi Germany, 1933–1943.* Tübingen: Mohr Siebeck, 1986.

Pearlman, Moshe. *The Capture and Trial of Adolf Eichmann.* New York: Simon and Schuster, 1963.

Perkins, Robert L., ed. *History and System: Hegel's Philosophy of History.* Albany: State University of New York Press, 1984.

Peskowitz, Miriam, and Laura Levitt, eds. *Judaism Since Gender.* New York: Routledge, 1997.

Pinsker, Leon. *Autoemancipation: Mahnruf an seine Stammesgenossen.* Berlin: Commissions- Verlag von W. Issleib, 1882.

Poliakov, Leon. *L'Auberge des musiciens: Mémoires.* Paris: Mazarine, 1981.

———. *Harvest of Hate: The Nazi Program for the Destruction of the Jews of Europe.* Westport, Conn.: Greenwood, 1954.

Pollock, Benjamin. *Franz Rosenzweig's Conversions.* Bloomington: Indiana University Press, 2014.

Rakovsky, Puah. *My Life as a Radical Jewish Woman: Memoirs of a Zionist Feminist in Poland.* Edited with an introduction by Paula E. Hyman. Bloomington: Indiana University Press, 2002.

Ranke, Leopold von. *Englische Geschichte vornehmlich im siebzehnten Jahurhundert.* Leipzig: Duncker und Humblot, 1877.

Rapoport-Albert, Ada. "Hagiography with Footnotes: Edifying Tales and the Writing of History in Hasidism." *History and Theory* 27 (1988): 119–159.

Rawidowicz, Simon, ed. *Kitve Rabi Nachman Krochmal.* London: Ararat, 1971.

Richarz, Monika. *Der Eintritt der Juden in die Akademischen Berufe: Jüdische Studenten und Akademiker in Deutschland, 1678–1848.* Tübingen: Mohr, 1974.

Rieff, David. *In Praise of Forgetting: Historical Memory and Its Ironies.* New Haven: Yale University Press, 2016.

Ringelblum, Emmanuel. *Ketavim aharonim.* Edited by Israel Gutman, Yosef Kormish, and Israel Shaham. Jerusalem: Yad Vashem: 1994.

———. *Notes from the Warsaw Ghetto: The Journal of Emmanuel Ringelblum.* Edited and translated by Jacob Sloan. New York: Schocken, 1974.

Roemer, Nils H. *Jewish Scholarship and Culture in Nineteenth-Century Germany: Between History and Faith.* Madison: University of Wisconsin Press, 2005.

Roskies, David G. *Against the Apocalypse: Responses to Catastrophe in Modern Jewish Culture.* Cambridge: Harvard University Press, 1984.

———. *The Jewish Search for a Usable Past.* Bloomington: Indiana University Press, 1999.

Roskies, David G., ed. *Literature of Destruction: Jewish Responses to Catastrophe.* Philadelphia: Jewish Publication Society, 1988.

Rosman, Moshe. *How Jewish Is Jewish History?* Oxford: Littman Library of Jewish Civilization, 2007.

Rousso, Henri. *The Haunting Past: History, Memory, and Justice in Contemporary France.* Translated by Ralph Schoolcraft. Philadelphia: University of Pennsylvania Press, 2002.

Rozenblit, Marsha L. *Reconstructing a National Identity: The Jews of Habsburg Austria During World War I.* Oxford: Oxford University Press, 2001.

Salfeld, Siegmund, ed. *Das Martyrologium des Nürnberger Memorbuches.* Berlin: Leonhard Simion, 1898.

Schonberger, Howard. "Purposes and Ends in History: Presentism and the New Left." *History Teacher* 7 (1974): 448–458.

Schorsch, Ismar. *From Text to Context: The Turn to History in Modern Judaism.* Hanover, N.H.: Brandeis University Press, 1994.

———. *Leopold Zunz: Creativity in Adversity.* Philadelphia: University of Pennsylvania Press, 2016.

Schwarzbard, Samuel. *Mémoires d'un anarchiste juif.* Paris: Éditions Syllepse, 2010.

Scott, Joan. *Gender and the Politics of History.* New York: Columbia University Press, 1988.

Segev, Tom. *The Seventh Million: The Israelis and the Holocaust.* Translated by Haim Watzman. New York: Hill and Wang, 1993.

Shtif, Nokhem. "Vegn a yidishn akademishn institute." In *Di organizatsye fun der yiddisher visnshaft.* Vilna: TSBK and VILBIG, 1925.

Sieg, Ulrich. *Germany's Prophet: Paul Lagarde and the Origins of Modern Antisemitism.* Translated by Linda Ann Marianiello. Waltham, Mass.: Brandeis University Press, 2013.

Silberstein, Laurence J. *The Postzionism Debates: Knowledge and Power in Israeli Culture.* New York: Routledge, 1999.

Smith, Bonnie G. *The Gender of History: Men, Women, and Historical Practice.* Cambridge: Harvard University Press, 1998.

Smith, Mark S. "The Yiddish Historians and the Struggle for a Jewish History of the Holocaust," Ph.D. diss., University of California, Los Angeles, 2016.

Snyder, Timothy D. *Black Earth: The Holocaust as History and Warning.* New York: Tim Duggan Books, 2015.

Stangneth, Bettina. *Eichmann Before Jerusalem: The Unexamined Life of a Mass Murderer.* New York: Vintage, 2015.

Stein, Arlene. *Reluctant Witnesses: Survivors, Their Children, and the Rise of Holocaust Consciousness.* Oxford: Oxford University Press, 2014.

Steinberg, Aaron, ed. *Simon Dubnow: The Man and His Work.* Paris: World Jewish Congress, 1963.

Stern, Selma. *The Court Jew: A Contribution to the History of the Period of Absolutism in Central Europe.* Translated by Ralph Weiman. Philadelphia: Jewish Publication Society of America, 1950.

Stolow, Jeremy. *Orthodoxy by Design: Judaism, Print Politics, and the ArtScroll Revolution.* Berkeley: University of California Press, 2010.

Sutcliffe, Adam. *Judaism and Enlightenment.* Cambridge: Cambridge University Press, 2003.

Taberner, Stuart, and Frank Finlay, eds. *Recasting German Identity: Culture, Politics, and Literature in the Berlin Republic.* Rochester, N.Y.: Camden Hill, 2002.

Tcherikower, Elias. "Jewish Martyrology and Jewish Historiography." *YIVO Annual of Jewish Social Science* 1 (1946): 9–23.

Toews, John E. "Intellectual History After the Linguistic Turn: The Autonomy of Meaning and the Irreducibility of Experience." *American Historical Review* 92 (1987): 879–907.

Trachtenberg, Barry. *The Revolutionary Roots of Modern Yiddish, 1903–1917.* Syracuse, N.Y.: Syracuse University Press, 2008.

Tupper, Frederick. "The Consolation of History: An After Dinner Speech at the Annual Banquet of the Vermont Commandery of the Loyal Legion of the United States," May 11, 1920 (n.p.).

Turner, Mathew. "Historians as Expert Witnesses: How Do Holocaust Perpetrator Trials Shape Historiography?" Alfred Deakin Research Institute Working Paper 22, November 2011, 5–12.

Thackeray, H. St. John. *Josephus: The Man and the Historian.* New York: Ktav, 1967.

Tosh, John. *Historians on History: An Anthology.* Harlow, U.K.: Pearson Education, 2000.

Usque, Samuel. *Consolation for the Tribulations of Israel.* Translated by Martin A. Cohen. Philadelphia: Jewish Publication Society of America, 1977.

Vidal-Naquet, Pierre. "Derrière le miroir." *Pensée de midi* 3 (2000): 10–20.

Wallach, Luitpold. *Liberty and Letters: The Thoughts of Leopold Zunz.* London: East and West Library, 1959.

Walzer, Michael. *Exodus and Revolution.* New York: Basic, 1985.

Weber, Elisabeth. *Questioning Judaism: Interviews by Elisabeth Weber.* Stanford, Calif.: Stanford University Press, 2004.

Wein, Berel. *Triumph of Survival: The Story of the Jews in the Modern Era, 1650–1990.* Brooklyn, N.Y.: Shaar Press with Mesorah Publications, 1990.

Weissler, Chava. *Voices of the Matriarchs.* Boston: Beacon, 1998.

Weitz, Yechiam, ed. *Ben hazon le-revizyah: me'ah shenot historiyografyah Tsionit.* Jerusalem: Zalman Shazar Center, 1997.

White, Hayden. "The Question of Narrative in Contemporary Historical Theory." *History and Theory* 23 (1984): 12–14.

Wiener, Max, comp. *Abraham Geiger and Liberal Judaism: The Challenge of the Nineteenth Century.* Translated by Ernst J. Schlochauer. Philadelphia: Jewish Publication Society of America, 1962.

Wieviorka, Annette. *The Era of the Witness.* Translated by Jared Stark. Ithaca: Cornell University Press, 2006.

Winter, Jay, and Emmanuel Sivan, eds. *War and Remembrance in the Twentieth Century.* Cambridge: Cambridge University Press, 1999.

Wyschogrod, Edith. *An Ethics of Remembering: History, Heterology, and the Nameless Others.* Chicago: University of Chicago Press, 1998.

Yablonka, Hanna. *The State of Israel vs. Adolf Eichmann.* Translated by Ora Cummings. New York: Schocken, 2004.

Yedidya, Asaf. *Legadel tarbut 'Ivriyah: hayav u-mishnato shel Zeev Jawitz.* Jerusalem: Mosad Bialik, 2016.

Yerushalmi, Yosef Hayim. *Freud's Moses: Judaism Terminable and Interminable.* New Haven: Yale University Press, 1991.

———. *Zakhor: Jewish History and Jewish Memory.* Rev. ed., New York: Schocken, 1989.

Young, James E. "Between History and Memory: The Uncanny Voices of Historian and Survivor." *History and Memory* 9, nos. 1–2 (1997): 47–58.

Zertal, Idith. *Israel's Holocaust and the Politics of Nationhood.* Translated by Chaya Galai. Cambridge: Cambridge University Press, 2005.

Zerubavel, Eviatar. *Time Maps: Collective Memory and the Social Shape of the Past.* Chicago: University of Chicago Press, 2003.

Zim, Rivkah. *Consolations of Writing: Literary Strategies of Resistance from Boethius to Primo Levi.* Princeton: Princeton University Press, 2014.

Zimmels, H. J. *Leopold Zunz: His Life and Times.* London: Jewish Religious Educational Publications, 1952.

Zinn, Howard. *Howard Zinn on History.* New York: Seven Stories, 2001.

———. *You Can't Be Neutral on a Moving Train: A Personal History of Our Times.* Boston: Beacon, 1994.

Zuckermann, Moshe. *Sho'ah ba-ḥeder ha-aṭum: ha-"Sho'ah" ba-'itonut ha-Yisre'elit bi-teḳufat Milḥemet ha-Mifrats.* Tel Aviv: Moshe Zuckermann, 1993.

Zunz, Leopold. *Gesammelte Schriften.* Vol. 1. Berlin: Verlag Louis Lamm. 1919.

———. *Ha-derashot be-Yisra'el.* Edited by Hanoch Albeck. Jerusalem: Mosad Bialik, 1974.

———. *Namen der Juden: Eine geschichtliche Untersuchung.* Leipzig: L. Fort, 1837.

INDEX

Adams, Hannah, 26–27, 30, 56, 62
advisory function of history, 111–112
Adwan, Sami, 107
African Americans: and historical memory, 6; reparations for slavery, 111, 153n30
Against Apion (Josephus), 56, 57
Agnon, S. Y., 70
Akiba, Rabbi, 58
Allison, Graham, 112
American history, rewriting, 6, 24
Annales school, 51
Antiochus IV Epiphanes, 67
Antisemiţism un pogromen in Ukraine, 1917–1918, 80
Applied History Project, Harvard University, 112
Aquarianism, 12
Arafat, Yasir, 107
Arendt, Hannah, 91, 93
Armenian-Turkish conflict, 106
Armitage, David, 112, 120n8
ArtScroll imprint, 35
Ashkenazic Jewry: Crusader violence against, 57–58, 66; martyrdom ideal for, 58–59
assimilation, 68–69
Assmann, Aleida, 17
Assmann, Jan, 17
Association for Jewish Studies, 125–126n45

Auerbach, Rachel, 85
Avineri, Shlomo, 63

Baer, Yitzhak (Fritz): *Galut,* 14–15, 42, 70; as Hispanist, 43; nationalism of, 42–43
banality of evil, 91
Barbie, Klaus, 92
Barkan, Elazar, 153n28
Bar-On, Dan, 107
Baron, Salo W., 33, 66, 115; Eichmann trial testimony of, 86–92; on "historical *midrash,*" 134n2; lachrymose theory of, 61, 67; on methodology, 155n2; on political activism of Jewish scholars, 39
Barth, Jakob, 33
Barthes, Roland, 115–116
Baskin, Judith, 49
Basnage, Jacques, 25–26, 30, 56, 62
Beard, Charles, 156n10
Becker, Carl, 156n10
Beer, Peter, 29–30
Begin, Menachem, 103
Ben-Gurion, David, 44, 86, 87, 88, 90, 91, 103
Berliner, Abraham, 33
Bernfeld, Shimon, 66–68
Bérubé, Michael, 3
Bialik, Chaim Nachman, 70, 79, 88
biblical prophets, as consolers, 55

Black Earth (Snyder), 100
Bloch, Marc, 1–2, 4, 15, 20, 113
blood libel, 137n19
Bloxham, Donald, 84
Blumenberg, Hans, 138n28
Boethius, 52, 135n3
Book of Tears, 66–68
Borges, Jorge Luis, 9
Boyarin, Daniel, 37
brain research, 148–149n7
Braudel, Fernand, 17
Brenner, Michael, 34, 37, 122n17
Broszat, Martin, 86
Brot, Rivka, 145
Browning, Christopher, 94
Brown v. Board of Education, 82
Buber, Martin, 70
Buchheim, Hans, 86
Buruma, Ian, 93
Butler, Judith, 109
Butterfield, Herbert, 22

Caligula, emperor, 56
Chauncey, George, 82
Chazan, Robert, 124n28
Chmielnicki mass murders, 59
Christianity: forcible conversion
    to, 59; and liberation historiog-
    raphy, 26–28
Chronicle of Higher Education, 3
Coates, Ta-Nehisi, 153n30
Cohen, Hermann, 81
Cohen, Martin, 59
collective memory, 5; decay of, 8–9;
    and modern Jewish historians,
    65; reverential, 36–37; in social
    network, 54–55; in traditional
    religion, 10–11; in *Zakhor*, 17, 102.
    See also memory, historical
collective remembrance, 136n11

Collingwood, R. G., 18, 78, 117–118,
    156n13
commissions of inquiry, 85, 144n18
consolation, Jewish: biblical
    sources of, 55; historiography as,
    70, 71–73; and history of hope,
    51–53; and Jewish survival, 63–70;
    of Josephus, 56; lachrymose
    theory of, 61–62; and martyrdom
    ideal, 58–59; modes of writing,
    52; preexisting patterns of mem-
    ory in, 54–55, 58–59; submis-
    sion to God's power in, 55–56;
    Usque's *Consolation*, 59–61
*Consolation for the Tribulations of
    Israel* (Usque), 59, 61
Consolation of Israel (Buber and
    Rosensweig), 70
Consolation of Philosophy (Boethius),
    135n3
Contemporary Relevance of History
    (Baron), 115
conversions, forcible, 59
Cott, Nancy, 82
Court Jew (Stern), 73
court testimony, historians', 79;
    Barbie trial, 92; Eichmann trial,
    86–92, 93; function of, 97–98, 99;
    German historians in war crim-
    inal cases, 85–86; Lipstadt libel
    trial, 94–96, 97–98; Nuremberg
    trials, 84–85; Papon trial, 92–93; in
    Petliura assassination trial, 83–84;
    Rousso's objection to, 92–93,
    96–97, 153n28; in United States, 83
Cover, Robert, 77–78, 100
Croce, Benedetto, 117
Crusades, chronicles of, 57–58, 64,
    66, 67, 137n19
cycles of history concept, 62–64, 73

da Costa, Uriel, 29–30
Damasio, Antonio, 149n7
Dangerous Games: The Uses and Abuses of History (MacMillan), 7
Denying the Holocaust (Lipstadt), 94, 97–98
Derenbourg, Joseph, 31
DiGioia, John J., 111
Dilthey, Wilhelm, 10, 127n1
Dinur, Ben Zion, 42, 43–44, 45
"Discourse of History" (Barthes), 115–116
Douglas, Lawrence, 91, 97
Dubnow, Simon, 33, 34, 74; on Crusader violence, 66; death of, 80; on Jewish survival, 68–70; in secular nationalist movement, 39–41; witnessing by, 79–81, 83
Du Pisani, Jacobus, 153n28
Dworzecki, Mark, 72, 85

Eban, Abba, 103
Eichmann in Jerusalem (Arendt), 91
Eichmann trial, 86–92, 93
Einstein, Albert, 88
Eliav, Benjamin, 86
Eliezer bar Nathan, 58
Elkana, Yehuda, 103, 104
emancipation of the Jews, 39, 65
Emmanuel, Isaac, 71
Engel, David, 61
England, Richard, 104–105
Enlightenment, 61, 62, 63
Equal Employment Opportunities Commission (EEOC) v. Sears, 82–83, 144n20
ethical function of history, 110–111
Evans, Richard, Lipstadt libel trial testimony of, 94, 95–96, 97, 99, 101

exceptionalism, and Jewish survival, 63–70
Exodus and Revolution (Walzer), 23
Exodus story, 23
expert witness, 82–83

Faust, Drew Gilpin, 153n30
Ferguson, Niall, 112
fictional/historical narratives, 118
"Folktales of Justice" (Cover), 77
forgetting trauma-induced memories, 102–104
Franklin, John Hope, 6, 82, 120–121n10
Franz Rosenzweig Lectures, Yale University, 13
Freud, Sigmund, 13–14
Freud's Moses (Yerushalmi), 15, 124
Friedlander, Saul, 16, 17, 76, 103, 125n40
Friedman, Philip, 85
Friedman, Thomas, 151–152n21
Friedrich Wilhelm III, king of Prussia, 38
From Slavery to Freedom (Franklin), 6
Funes the Memorious (fictional character in Borges), 9
Funkenstein, Amos, 11
Furet, François, 17
Fussell, Paul, 53

Gaddis, John Lewis, 132n43
Galut (Baer), 14–15, 42, 70
Garbarini, Alexandra, 80
Gay, Peter, 15
Geary, Patrick, 6, 121n11
Geiger, Abraham, 30–32
Gender and Assimilation in Modern Jewish History (Hyman), 49

Jewish historiography (*continued*)
audience, 33–37; periodization
of, 31–32; in postwar Germany,
19, 126n46; purposes of, 19–20;
Schocken Bücherei series, 70;
and secular bias, 33–34; Spanish,
14–15, 124n35; validation of,
28; Warsaw Ghetto, 71–73; of
Wissenschaft des Judentums,
27, 28, 31, 33, 34, 37, 40, 41, 42,
45, 65–66; women's history,
46–49; in Yiddish, 45–46. *See also*
consolation, Jewish; liberation,
historiographical; witnessing,
historical
Jewish War (Josephus), 56
*Jewish Women in Historical Perspec-
tive* (Baskin, ed.), 49
Job, 55
Josephus, Flavius, 25, 55–56, 57
Judge and the Historian (Ginzburg),
77, 101
Judt, Tony, 109
Julius, Anthony, 94
"Just One Witness" (Ginzburg),
76, 77

Kabbalah, 42, 44
Karaism, 30
Kassow, Samuel D., 71
Kermish, Yosef, 85
Kessler-Harris, Alice, 82–83,
144n20
Kim, Kwang-Su, 153n28
Kishinev pogroms (1903), 79
Klausner, Yosef, 34, 41
kosher meat boycott, 48
Krausnick, Helmut, 86
Krochmal, Nachman, 63–65
Kurzweil, Baruch, 121n13

LaCapra, Dominick, 17
lachrymose theory of Jewish his-
tory, 61–62, 67, 86
Lagarde, Paul de, 81
Lamed-Vov Tsadikim (36 Righ-
teous Ones), 88
Landau, Moshe, 87, 88
Landmann, Michael, 126n46
Langer, Lawrence, 17
Latvia, Nazi massacre of Jews in, 80
legal witnessing, 76–78. *See also*
court testimony, historians'
Lepage Center for History in the
Public Interest, 154n35
Lerner, Gerda, 3–4, 24, 47–48
Leschnitzer, Adolf, 126n46
Lestshinsky, Jacob, 46
Levi, Primo, 76
liberation, historiographical:
catalysts for, 23–24, 37; Christian,
25–28; and Exodus story, 23; and
Jerusalem historians, 41–46; and
Jewish revitalization, 30–33; in
Jewish studies, 27–29; and polit-
ical emancipation, 37–39; from
rabbinic authority, 23, 29–30;
from secular bias, 33–37; and
secular nationalism, 39–41; from
Wissenschaft des Judentums, 41,
42; and women's history, 46–49
Lieux de mémoire (Nora), 10
Life of Jesus (Strauss), 31
Lipstadt, Deborah, libel trial of,
94–96, 97–98, 99, 101
*Living with History/Making Social
Change* (Lerner), 24
Longerich, Peter, 94
Löwith, Karl, 62
Luskin Center for History and
Policy, 154n36